# The **Skinny Instant Pot** Cookbook

## Cook Yourself Skinny with the Easiest + Most Delicious
## 400-Calorie Recipes for Your Instant Pot Pressure Cooker

*by Lauren Smythe*

The health advice presented in this book is intended only as an informative resource guide to help you make informed decisions; it is not meant to replace the advice of a physician or to serve as a guide to self-treatment. Always seek competent medical help for any health condition or if there is any question about the appropriateness of a procedure or health recommendation.

Always follow safety and commonsense cooking protocol while using kitchen utensils, operating ovens, stoves, and appliances, and handling uncooked food. If children are assisting in the preparation of any recipe, they should always be supervised by an adult.

# The Skinny Instant Pot Cookbook

# Want to help us spread the word about low-calorie living?

## Leave a review on Amazon!

A review is the best way to help spread the word about how easy it is to eat healthy and low-calorie, and hopefully it will help the next person find their way to healthier, easier low-calorie Instant Pot meals, too!

**To leave a review:**

Copy this URL into your browser: http://bit.ly/skinnyinstantpot

OR

Google search "Skinny Instant Pot Cookbook Lauren Smythe" and click the first Amazon link.

This should take you to the Amazon book page, where you can leave a review.

**Thank you so much!**

# The **Skinny Instant Pot** Cookbook

## The Easiest + Most Delicious 400-Calorie Recipes for Your Instant Pot

## Table of Contents

# Low-Calorie Instant Pot Recipes by Category

Sometimes what I need most on busy nights is **the right recipe at the right time**. Maybe you do, too? Here are all the low-calorie Instant Pot recipes in this book, grouped by their category, so that you can find a 20-minute recipe for when everyone is hangry, a 7-ingredient recipe for when you haven't had time to grocery shop, and a kid-friendly recipe for those cranky nights.

I hope you find that the Instant Pot electric pressure cooker is just what you need to make your new low-calorie lifestyle easy, fun, and delicious!

# Kid-Friendly Recipes

# 7 Ingredients or Less Recipes

# 20 Minutes or Less Recipes

# Introduction

I was never a person who watched everything I ate or counted calories. I grew up eating footlong subs in the school cafeteria, pizza every Friday night, and sugary cereal with my cartoons on Saturday morning. In college, I was right there along with the rest of my friends, drinking beer, ordering late night pizza, and never worrying about my weight or how food made my body feel-- because I was young and could get away with it.

But as I got older, I noticed that fried food sat heavier in my stomach, and that all those cans of soda and sugary snacks were starting to pack on the weight. Then I had a daughter and life got even busier. Soon, I realized my jeans were a little tighter and my motivation was a little lower each day. Just as bad, I felt SO tired all the time. It was difficult enough to get through my to-do list each day and take care of my family, and I just couldn't seem to find the time or energy to go to the gym.

Feeling depressed that my health was always being pushed to the backburner, I finally caved and bought *The Skinnytaste Cookbook: Light on Calories and Big on Flavor* by Gina Homolka.

I'd heard a lot about how counting calories helps you lose weight, but I didn't know if it was necessarily for me at first. That all changed when I spoke with a few close friends who were all starting a 30-day low-calorie diet together. They couldn't stop raving about how much better they felt. And when I realized that my friends—who were just as busy and stretched thin as I was—were suddenly healthier, thinner, and more energetic than I'd seen them in years, I realized that I needed to do whatever they were doing, and quick.

My husband and I decided to try restricting our calories for a few weeks, just to see how it went. And to our disbelief, **it totally changed us**. We started thinking about food differently, and we couldn't believe how good avoiding fried, processed, and calorie-packed food made us feel. We felt younger, stronger, and happier than we had in years.

But after the first few weeks of our new low-calorie lifestyle, we started missing our favorite foods, like buffalo wings and tacos. We were tired of low-cal wraps and yogurts every day, but we didn't want to go back to our old ways, which left us feeling bloated and exhausted after dinner.

We also loved that we were cooking and eating together as a family more, and my daughter was already less stressed and more interested in what was going on in the kitchen. But since we were trying to avoid calorie-packed takeout and dining out, we needed quicker and easier recipes to make at home every night. And on top of that, we needed them to be kid-friendly *and* low-calorie. Sounds like a tall order, right?

Around that time, I received an Instant Pot electric pressure cooker as a gift from my mom, who is an incredible cook and is obsessed with her Instant Pot. **That was a big breakthrough for us as a family:** the Instant Pot allowed us to do hands-off, low-calorie cooking, all while spending less time in the kitchen and *still* steadily losing weight. In fact, I've lost 25 pounds since getting my Instant Pot and starting to cook these recipes! If that's not a win-win-win, I don't know what is.

Now, dinner at my house looks like this: I toss a few ingredients in the Instant Pot, set it to electric pressure cooking mode, then hang out in the living room, catching up with my husband or helping the kids with their homework. No more watching and stirring over the stove or peeking and prodding in the oven!

I hope you enjoy this collection of skinny Instant Pot recipes as much as my family has. My wish is that this book makes you and your family healthier and happier, one meal at a time.

**If you do find these recipes helpful, would you consider leaving a review on Amazon?** It would mean so much to me and will hopefully help the next person find their way to an easier, healthier time in the kitchen! (To leave a review, type this link to your browser: http://bit.ly/skinnyinstantpot or go to the Amazon page where you bought this book.)

Thank you so much for purchasing this book, and happy cooking!

Lauren

# Part II: A Low-Calorie Diet + The Instant Pot = A Match Made in Heaven

# About the Low-Calorie Instant Pot Recipes in this Book

The low-calorie recipes in this book are designed with real families in mind: the kind who want to eat whole, real food, but also need to keep dinner quick, easy, and affordable. Every recipe is 400 calories or less, and many are grain-free and dairy-free, but you'll hardly miss those with all the delicious veggies packed in each meal!

Within these pages you'll find my very favorite low-calorie Instant Pot recipes. You can also make these recipes using another brand of electric pressure cooker, but please note that settings and cooking times may vary, so consult the manual for your particular electric pressure cooker.

These low-calorie Instant Pot recipes are the keepers that I turn to again and again, and here's why I think you'll love them, too:

## Each low-calorie Instant Pot recipe aims for:

- **Easy-to-find, affordable ingredients:** You won't find any expensive or unpronounceable ingredients here. While there are a few key swaps I'll walk you through that will help you get the most bang from each calorie, I make sure they get used over and over in other recipes, so you're not stuck with an ingredient you'll never use again. (I hate that!)

- **Kid-friendly, adaptable recipes:** My kids are super picky eaters, so I always create recipes with them in mind. These low-calorie Instant Pot recipes are as simple as they can be while still being flavorful. Even better, each recipe says whether it's especially kid-friendly, and where possible, I included suggestions for how to adapt the recipe for both adult and kid taste buds.

  Remember, these recipes are designed to serve as templates for everything that's possible with your Instant Pot, so never hesitate to skip or substitute flavoring ingredients like spices or sauces if your kiddos don't like them!

- **7 Ingredient or Less recipes:** If you're like me and don't want to spend tons of time pulling ingredients from cabinets and measuring them, these low-calorie Instant Pot recipes are for you! The recipes will point out if it's a 7 Ingredient or Less recipe (not including salt and pepper, of course). That way, you can easily turn to those recipes on nights when you want to keep things simple. (Hellooo, Wednesday night soccer practice.)

- **20 Minutes or Less recipes:** The beauty of the Instant Pot electric pressure cooker is that it's hands-free cooking, and it's incredibly fast. I've highlighted the recipes that are 20 Minutes or Less to cook once at pressure, so you can quickly turn to those when you have cranky kids or a hangry husband to feed. (Basically every night in my house…)

# 3 Hacks for Better Instant Pot Cooking

After experimenting with the Instant Pot electric pressure cooker for over a year, I've learned a few hacks that make the best use of this handy new appliance. I use these almost every single time I make a low-calorie Instant Pot recipe, and they've saved me hundreds of hours in the kitchen and have resulted in more flavorful meals.

**1. Thicken the sauce, if you have the time.**

Because the Instant Pot always needs to have about 1 cup of liquid in it for the food to steam correctly, you'll get delicious broths and sauces with nearly every meal. (Bonus: these broths and sauces are typically low-calorie *and* they'll make you feel satisfied!)

But sometimes, you might find that you have too much liquid after cooking, and that it's a bit thin. Sauté setting to the rescue! If I have time, I'll often remove the food from the Instant Pot, leaving the sauce, and then set the pot on high heat on the Sauté setting. You can let it cook down as much as you want, or add a thickener to make it more like a gravy. A great low-calorie thickener you probably already have in your pantry is cornstarch or all-purpose flour. But if you're avoiding grains, you can also try arrowroot powder. I love Starwest Botanicals brand Organic Arrowroot Powder, which you can find at specialty food stores or online at this link: http://bit.ly/starwestarrowroot.

> **To make a thickener:**
> Whisk 1 teaspoon cornstarch, flour, or arrowroot powder into 2 tablespoons water, broth, or sauce.
> Slowly whisk into the pot and allow to cook until thickened.

**2. Use the pocket of time during pressure cooking to make a side.**

When I first start looking for Instant Pot recipes, it seemed like many of them had you first cook the protein, then empty the pot and cook a vegetable side. Yikes—I don't have time for that! If you don't either, here's what I suggest: get your Instant Pot recipe locked and loaded, then use the time during pressure cooking to toss together quick roasted vegetables, spiralize some carrots, or microwave a few baked sweet potatoes.

My favorite low-calorie vegetable side is a big tray of brussels sprouts, cauliflower, or broccoli, which I cook under the broiler instead of roasting to save even more time.

> **To make quick and easy broiled vegetables:**
> Toss 1-inch pieces of any oven-friendly vegetable with 1 tablespoon olive oil, 1 tablespoon stock, salt, and pepper.
> Place under the broiler until crispy, watching carefully so they don't burn.

**3. Taste your food before serving and add more salt and pepper, if necessary.**

We all like our food at different levels of saltiness and pepperiness, so please always take my measurements as a suggestion, not a rule! This is especially true of Instant Pot recipes, since you're often using broth as the steaming liquid. Different brands of broth have vastly different salt content, so if you're unsure how salty your broth might be, use less salt before pressure cooking. You can always add more salt and pepper once you open up the pot again!

# Chapter 2: Why Low Calorie?

Calories in, calories out. Have you heard that weight loss theory? It may sound simplistic in this age of confusing diets, fasting, and gluten-free-everything, but the science is incontrovertible: a low-calorie diet increases weight loss and life span and decreases the chances of suffering from a diet-related illness, such as diabetes or heart-disease.

However, most Americans eat way too many calories—the standard American diet centers around fried food, fast food, frozen food, processed food, and every other kind of "food" that isn't actually food. I know it, because I lived it! But eating too many calories and not burning them off leads to weight gain, more stress on your body, and a higher risk for disease.

So a low-calorie diet is designed to help you re-learn exactly how much energy—a.k.a. calories—your body really needs to feel great. Once you've found that perfect place of *enough*, your body will naturally stay at a healthy weight, you'll feel more focused and energetic, and you'll sleep longer and more soundly. Sounds pretty great, right?

But it's easy to trick yourself into believing that you're eating right if you don't track exactly what you eat. Suddenly, your cheat day will become a cheat *week*, and you'll feel frustrated and guilty that you're not losing weight like you swore you would. That's when it's time to step back and commit to tracking your daily calorie intake, so you can take control of your life and your health, instead of letting food control you.

By seeing how we feel when we cut high-calorie, processed foods from our diets, we can finally—usually for the first time in our lives—see how our bodies feel when we fill them only with real, nourishing food.

# How to Stick to a Low-Calorie Diet

Believe it or not, it can be easy to stick to a low-calorie diet. Yes, you heard that right. Easy.

But you've probably heard stories of people falling off the diet wagon after a few days, or gaining all the weight back after following a crazy new fad diet for a few weeks.

Most people fail at a low-calorie diet for two reasons:

1. They're not eating the right foods.
2. They're *overly* restricting their calorie intake.

Studies have shown that the over-restriction of calories leads to fatigue, and you oftentimes fail to meet your daily nutrient needs; cutting out too many calories ends up cutting out the important vitamins and nutrients, too. In particular, relying on processed foods that are marketed as low-calorie is a big trap many people fall into.

When my husband and I first started counting calories, we stocked up on low-calorie frozen dinners, snacks, yogurt, and every other "healthy" thing we could find at the store. But an hour or two after eating our low-calorie frozen dinners, we felt hungry. Why?

We were eating all the wrong foods.

Most products marketed as low-calorie are packed with empty carbs and sugar and devoid of protein and fiber. But guess what? Protein and fiber are what make you feel full. Yes, carbs and sugar will temporarily satisfy you, but in reality, they are merely spiking your blood sugar. And once it drops, you'll feel hungrier than ever.

That's why it's important to set a calorie goal that isn't too extreme and to make sure you're eating a diet heavy in protein and vegetables. Doctors usually recommend starting with a 25% restriction of your daily calories so that it doesn't become unhealthy, but please consult your own physician before making any major changes to your diet.

# My Secret Weapon for Staying Motivated

In order to make sure you're losing weight in a healthy way, it's important to eat just the right amount of calories: not too many and not too few. So how do you determine how many calories you should be eating based on your weight loss goals?

Calculator.net has a calories calculator that takes into account your age, height, weight, gender, and weekly exercise to determine how many calories you need daily to maintain, lose, or gain weight. Typically, cutting 500 calories per day will help you lose one pound a week, but this will vary drastically based on your body type and activity level. Doctors recommend losing no more than two pounds a week, because anything beyond that is decidedly unhealthy. (And remember: restricting your calories too much is a recipe for following off the wagon!)

To help you stick to your diet, doctors recommend keeping an accurate diary of your food. By keeping yourself accountable in writing, you'll easily be able to see how much more you were eating than your body needed, and then just as easily adjust to what's right for you.

But lugging around a written food journal just didn't work with my busy life, so my secret weapon has become the My Fitness Pal app. My Fitness Pal lets you set your weight loss goals, track your food and exercise, and keep you motivated by giving you a virtual high-five when you're on a streak of tracking for several days in a row. MyFitnessPal also has a huge archive of popular foods in its search function, so rather than trudging into the kitchen to check how many calories were in that tortilla, you can search by exact brand name and product.

In addition to keeping track of your intake, it's a good idea to write out menus for the week. This helps you stay on track in advance, and gives you a plan for those unexpectedly busy evenings! Having a menu in place will prevent you from giving in and stopping for fast food, which was my go-to whenever I felt too stressed to cook.

In the end, following a low-calorie diet has benefits for everyone, regardless of their weight loss goals. Cutting out heavy, calorie-loaded food will not just lower the number on the scale; it'll make you feel better, happier, and more focused in your daily life.

# High-Calorie Foods to Watch Out For

Besides the obvious high-calorie foods to avoid that offer no nutritional value (sorry, ice cream!), there are also some foods that you may think are healthy or natural that don't fit into your low-calorie diet.

Of course, no foods are completely off-limits, because the beauty of a low-calorie diet is that you can eat anything as long as it's within your calorie limit for the day. But it's important to remember that cutting calories works the best if you focus on balance and filling up on vegetables and lean proteins.

**Foods to avoid:**

- French Fries and potato chips
- Sugary drinks, such as bottled iced tea and Gatorade
- White bread
- Most fruit juices
- Pastries, cookies, and cake
- Peanut butter
- Chocolate
- Cheese
- Pasta
- Bacon, beef, and sausage
- Avocados
- Beer, red wine, and hard ciders
- Olive oil and other oils

# Low-Calorie Foods to Pile on Your Plate

On the other hand, here are some healthy whole foods to focus on as you put together meals for your family. Make these the focal point of your meals, and you'll never feel hungry even as the weight melts away!

- Chicken breast, turkey breast, pork tenderloin, and other white meats
- Salmon, cod, scallops, most seafood
- Cucumbers
- Bell peppers
- Mushrooms
- Spinach
- Kale
- Lettuce and all leafy greens
- Cabbage
- Berries

- Cantelope
- Watermelon
- Kiwi
- Citrus
- Black beans
- Lentils
- Skim milk
- Plain non-fat yogurt
- Eggs
- Shirataki noodles
- Oatmeal
- Wild rice
- Black coffee

**To read more about the low-calorie diet, I highly recommend these two books:**

*American Heart Association Low-Calorie Cookbook: More than 200 Delicious Recipes for Healthy Eating* by the American Heart Association

Use this link if you'd like to check out the *AHA Low-Calorie Cookbook*: http://bit.ly/AHACookbook.

*Quick & Easy Low Calorie Cookbook: 100 Recipes All 100 Calories 200 Calories 300 Calories* by Heather Thomas

Use this link if you'd like to check out *Quick & Easy Low Calorie*: http://bit.ly/Thomas100.

# Sanity-Saving Substitutions for Your Low-Calorie Pantry

While it may seem like some of your favorite foods might not fit into your low-calorie diet, once you get the hang of the substitutions, you'll see that you can still cook and enjoy many of your favorite recipes. With the right items in your low-calorie pantry, you'll quickly and easily be able to adapt your cooking to your healthy new life.

Today, there are low-calorie counterparts to almost everything. It's actually very easy to maintain a similar flavor profile in a recipe while stepping down its calorie count, as long as you make smart decisions at the grocery store.

So before you feel overwhelmed by all the low-calorie options out there, start with my quick guide to the best low-calorie products. Through much trial-and-error—and even a few ruined dinners!—I've finally found the low-calorie alternatives that taste and cook just like the real thing. I hope this saves you a lot of legwork, a few wasted dollars, and makes your transition to the low-calorie lifestyle easier and more delicious!

## My Favorite Swaps for a Low-Calorie Pantry

Instead of butter, **use an olive oil spray.**
> A spray makes it easy to coat a pan easily with much less fat than you would if you were taking pads from the butter dish.

> My favorite olive oil spray is Bertolli Extra Virgin Olive Oil Spray, found at http://bit.ly/BertolliSpray.

Instead of olive oil, **try a chicken or vegetable stock.**
> If you typically toss vegetables in oil before roasting, try cutting the quantity of oil in half and replacing it with your favorite stock.

> I like to use Pacific Foods Organic Low-Sodium Chicken Broth, found in many grocery stores and online at http://bit.ly/pacificchickenbroth and Imagine Organic Low-Sodium Vegetable Broth at http://bit.ly/ImagineBroth.

Instead of regular wheat bread, **try a low-calorie bread.**
> Just be sure it's one full of healthy whole grains, so it will leave you feeling satisfied.

> The Ezekiel 4:9 brand is my favorite (it's easy to find here: http://bit.ly/Ezekiel49Loaf), but Nature's Own 100% Whole Wheat is a cheaper option that is more available in stores.

Instead of pork bacon, **try turkey bacon.**
>Applegate has healthy and low calorie option that you might want to stock up on if you're a bacon lover: http://bit.ly/ApplegateTurkeyBacon.

Instead of regular pasta, switch to **spaghetti squash or zoodles**.
>Spaghetti squash is available at most grocery stores, and zoodles are easy to make using zucchini and a spiralizer. Spiralizers are affordable and easy to use; you can find a great one here: http://bit.ly/UltimateSpiralizer.

Or, if you like the texture of non-veggie noodles, switch to **shirataki noodles, low-carb noodles, or whole wheat noodles**.
>Shirataki noodles are (nearly) zero calorie noodles made from the fiber of the konjac plant, so they're also filling. They're growing in popularity, and the best brand is Miracle Noodles, which you can find here: http://bit.ly/MiracleShirataki.

>Dreamfields is my favorite brand of low-carb pasta (it will help you feel fuller with less!), and you can find it in many grocery stores and online here: http://bit.ly/DreamfieldsSpaghetti.

>Barilla also makes a great whole wheat pasta that's popular in stores and also easily bought online here: http://bit.ly/BarillaWheat.

Instead of hard cheese, **use low-calorie soft cheeses like feta and goat cheese.**
>A great grocery-store brand of feta cheese is Valbreso, which is made from sheep's milk. Cypress Grove has a delicious Humboldt Fog goat cheese, which you can purchase in many cheese markets and at http://bit.ly/HumboldtCheese.

**An important note on broth:**

Because of how the Instant Pot pressure cooks, it typically requires about 1 cup of liquid in the pot. You'll see that many of the recipes in this book call for chicken, beef, or vegetable broth, but please keep in mind that the quality of your broth will heavily influence the flavor of the final dish.

Try Bone Broth by Kettle & Fire, available at http://bit.ly/KettleFireBroth, for a top-of-the-line, just-like-homemade flavor.

Or for a more affordable, yet still delicious, option, try Pacific's organic, free-range line, on Amazon at http://bit.ly/pacificchickenbroth.

# Chapter 3: Understanding the Instant Pot Electric Pressure Cooker

The Instant Pot is America's #1 bestselling electric pressure cooker for a reason: it's so much more than a pressure cooker! The Instant Pot is a first-of-its kind multi-cooker, which combines a slow cooker, pressure cooker, and rice cooker into one handy electric appliance. Even better, the Instant Pot has a sauté function which allows you to brown vegetables, sear meat, and easily build flavor right in the pot, unlike traditional slow cookers or pressure cookers.

## Which Instant Pot model is right for you?

All of the Instant Pot models will have the basic buttons and functions you need to make every recipe in this book. However, there's a lot of variation from model to model, so here are a few tips for finding the Instant Pot electric pressure cooker that's right for you:

**If you want all 9 settings:**
> Get the Instant Pot DUO Plus 60 6 Quart 9-in-1 model here: http://bit.ly/instantpot9in1

**If you cook for a crowd:**
> Get the Instant Pot DUO80 7-in-1 in the 8 quart size here: http://bit.ly/instantpoteightqt

**If you have a small kitchen:**
> Get the Instant Pot DUO80 7-in-1 in the 3 quart size here: http://bit.ly/instantpot3qt

**If you're on a budget:**
> Get the Instant Pot LUX60 V3 6-in-1 in the 6 quart size here: http://bit.ly/instantpot6qt

## Which Instant Pot accessories are helpful?

While you don't need additional accessories to make any of the recipes in this book, you might find it helpful to have a few Instant Pot-friendly items to make things a little easier on yourself.

**For steaming vegetables, seafood, or delicate cuts of meat:**
> Instant Pot makes **a silicone steamer set,** available here, http://bit.ly/instantpotsteamerset, which makes it easier to use the Steam setting.

**For easily removing the trivet or pot without burning yourself:**
> Try Instant Pot's **silicone mini mitts,** which are practical, easy to store, and cute to boot! They can be found online here: http://bit.ly/instantpotminimitts

**For storing leftovers in your pot in the refrigerator:**

You can get a **silicone lid cover** here: http://bit.ly/instantpotsiliconelid. It fits snugly over your pot, saving you clean-up time after dinner.

**For doubling up on your pressure cooking:**

Get **an Instant Pot-approved backup pot**, for those times when you want to cook recipes back-to-back in your pot without doing dishes in between. Available online at http://bit.ly/instantpotinnerpot.

**For more Instant Pot recipes:**

I love *The Essential Instant Pot Cookbook* by Coco Morante and *Dinner in an Instant* by Melissa Clark.

Not all the recipes are low calorie, but you'll find great inspiration and you can modify many of the recipes to fit your new low calorie lifestyle.

You can find the *The Essential Instant Pot Cookbook* here: http://bit.ly/essentialinstantpot

You can find *Dinner in an Instant* here: http://bit.ly/DinnerInstant

# How does the Instant Pot pressure cook?

You may be coming to the Instant Pot with preconceived notions of what a pressure cooker is. Maybe you've heard stories about pressure cookers overflowing or spraying food everywhere, or maybe you remember the old-fashioned pressure cookers that loudly (and annoyingly) whistled.

Forget all those ideas; the Instant Pot is different. Because the Instant Pot is an *electric* pressure cooker that was specifically designed to be safer than stovetop pressure cookers, it has few of the issues of old-fashioned pressure cookers. But if you're like me and like to know how things work, you might be wondering how, exactly, the Instant Pot cooks food using the pressure cooking setting.

The Instant Pot electric pressure cooker program begins when you set the Pressure Release valve to "Sealing." From there, you select the program and set the desired time. The Instant Pot will give you 30-60 seconds to make your selections, and then it will automatically initiate the program.

As the Instant Pot begins to build heat, the pressure increases in the pot and the boiling point of the water or liquid in the pot also increases. As more and more steam is generated, the pressure continues to increase inside the pot. The water begins to reach a very high temperature, yet the high pressure and the increased boiling point prevents the water from boiling or evaporating.

The high-heat, high-moisture environment of the Instant Pot means you get exceptionally quick cooking times and incredibly moist food. Even typically dry cuts of meat, such as boneless skinless chicken breasts come out juicy and moist in just a few minutes. This makes it almost impossible to overcook or dry out your food—and who doesn't want that?!

# Inside Your Instant Pot Pressure Cooker

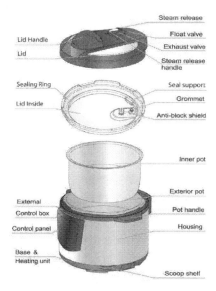

While other electric pressure cookers may have features that are different from the Instant Pot, almost all electric pressure cookers have several key parts:

**Inner pot.** Sometimes also referred to as the cooking pot. The inner pot is stainless steel, so it's easy to wash and can also be used to store leftovers in the refrigerator.

**Heating element.** The heating element is electric, meaning that you can plug in the pot and set it on your countertop, just like a slow cooker. This makes it perfect for small kitchens!

**Sensors.** The Instant Pot has several built-in pressure and temperature sensors that make it safer than a non electric pressure cooker. These sensors monitor the internal environment, maintain the desired cooking conditions, and help protect you from possible mishaps.

**Locking mechanism.** The Instant Pot has a sealing ring that creates a completely airtight chamber inside the pot so that steam can build up. Once you turn the pot lid to the Closed position, the vacuum seal is formed. The lid locks in place, so that you can't accidentally open the lid when the pot is at a high pressure.

**Push down pressure release:** The valves that are installed in the Instant Pot are designed with an innovative Anti-Block Shield that allows them to automatically react to changing conditions in the pot. The valves remain locked until the pressure goes beyond the specified threshold, at which point the valve pushes itself upward, slowly releasing the pressure and returning it to normal levels. These release valves are intelligently controlled with electronic sensors which automatically alter the settings depending on the type of food you're cooking.

# Understanding the Instant Pot Buttons

The Instant Pot is preprogrammed with various cooking settings, so that you can quickly and easily select the cooking program that's right for each kind of food. The Instant Pot company has spent years assimilating data from hundreds of chefs all over the world to arrive at these pre-programmed times, so the settings have a high level of accuracy.

Of course, a setting like "Bean" will only work if you have the recommended quantity of beans and liquid in the pot, so it's important to follow an Instant Pot recipe rather than just guess at the setting. You can also find comprehensive cooking times for basic ingredients in the Cooking Times for the Instant Pot Electric Pressure Cooker chart at the back of this book.

The Instant Pot comes in many models and sizes, so you may not have these exact buttons. If not, don't worry: you can always use the Manual or Pressure Cook setting to replicate the same results produced by the other buttons.

**Sauté:** Use this to sauté vegetables, sear meat, simmer a soup, thicken a sauce, or otherwise cook food over high heat like you would on the stovetop. This setting should only be used with the lid removed. Many Instant Pot models include buttons that allow you to adjust the heat to Low, Normal, or High, just as you would on the stovetop.

**Keep Warm/Cancel:** Use this button to turn your pressure cooker off or reset the cooking program. You can also use it to keep food warm in the Instant Pot until you're ready to serve it.

**Manual:** This is your go-to button for setting a cooking program. The manual button lets you set any cooking time at any pressure level, so it's a good back-up if your Instant Pot doesn't have a specific program called for in a recipe.

**Soup:** This will set the program to pressure cook, and you can adjust the time to 30 minutes of cooking time (at normal); 40 minutes (at more); 20 minutes (at less).

**Meat/Stew:** This will set the program to pressure cook, and you can adjust the time to 35 minutes of cooking time (at normal); 45 minutes (at more); 20 minutes (at less).

**Bean/Chili:** This will set the program to pressure cook, and you can adjust the time to 30 minutes of cooking time (at normal); 40 minutes (at more); 25 minutes (at less).

**Poultry:** This will set the program to pressure cook, and you can adjust the time to 15 minutes of cooking time (at normal); 30 minutes (at more); 5 minutes (at less).

**Rice:** This is a fully automated mode which allows you to easily cook rice on low pressure. It will adjust the timer automatically, depending on the amount of water and rice present inside the inner cooking pot.

**Multi-Grain:** This will set the program to pressure cook, and you can adjust the time to 40 minutes of cooking time (at normal); 45 minutes (at more); 20 minutes (at less).

**Porridge:** This will set the program to pressure cook, and you can adjust the time to 20 minutes of cooking time (at normal); 30 minutes (at more); 15 minutes (at less).

**Steam:** This setting is useful for quickly steaming vegetables, seafood, or thin cuts of meats. It will set your pressure cooker to high pressure with 10 minutes of cooking time (at normal); 15 minutes (at more); 3 minutes (at less). Use this setting with a steamer basket or trivet for best results, so that your food is elevated from the 1 cup of liquid that will also be in the pot.

**Slow Cooker:** This button will initiate the slow cooker function and set it for a 4-hour cook time. However, you can change the temperature—low will be at 190-201 degrees Fahrenheit; normal is 194-205 degrees Fahrenheit; high is 199-210 degrees Fahrenheit.

**Pressure:** This button allows you to switch between high and low-pressure settings.

**Yogurt:** This is an automatic setting that allows you to make yogurt in individual servings. Make sure you find a trustworthy, tested recipe for making yogurt using this function.

**Timer:** This button allows you to adjust the cooking time by pressing the + or – buttons.

# Part I:
# The Low-Calorie Instant Pot Recipes

# Low-Calorie Instant Pot Egg Recipes

# Foolproof Hard-Boiled and Soft-Boiled Eggs

Kid-Friendly
20 Minutes or Less
7 Ingredients or Less

Makes 2-12
Prep Time: 1 minute
Cook Time: 3-5 minutes

**Ingredients**
2-12 eggs (You can cook as many as fit in one layer in the pot)

**Directions**
Place the Instant Pot trivet inside the pot. Arrange eggs in one layer on top of the trivet and add 1 cup of water to the pot.

Lock the lid and set the Pressure Release to Sealing. Select the Pressure Cook or Manual setting and set the cooking time to 5 minutes for hard-boiled eggs or 3 minutes for soft-boiled eggs at high pressure.

Once the timer goes off, use a kitchen towel or oven mitts to protect your hand and move the Pressure Release knob to Venting to perform a quick pressure release.

Cool eggs under running water and peel.

Serving size: 1 large (50g) egg. Nutrition per serving: 77.5 calories, 5.3g fat (sat 1.6g), 212mg cholesterol, 6.3g protein, 0.6g total carbohydrate (0g fiber, 0.6g sugar), 62mg sodium

# Ham and Broccoli Crustless Quiche

Kid-Friendly
7 Ingredients or Less

Serves 2
Prep Time: 10 minutes
Cook Time: 30 minutes

**Ingredients**
6 large eggs
2 teaspoons unsalted butter, divided
½ cup extra lean, low-sodium ham, diced
½ cup broccoli florets, chopped small
1 green onion, chopped
¼ teaspoon salt
Pepper to taste

**Directions**
Place the trivet in the bottom of the Instant Pot and add 1 ½ cup of water to the pot. Grease a 1 quart round oven-safe dish (such as a casserole or soufflé dish) with 1 teaspoon of butter.

In a medium bowl, beat the eggs and add the remaining 1 teaspoon of butter, ham, broccoli, green onion, salt, and pepper. Stir well, then pour into the prepared dish.

Loosely cover the dish with aluminum foil and place inside the Instant Pot on top of the trivet. (Use an aluminum foil sling to lift in and out of the pot, if necessary.)

Lock the lid and set the Pressure Release to Sealing. Select the Pressure Cook or Manual setting and set the cooking time to 25 minutes at high pressure.

Once the timer goes off, let sit for at least 10 minutes; the pressure will release naturally. Then switch the Pressure Release to Venting to allow any last steam out.

Carefully remove the dish from the Instant Pot and serve warm.

**Note:** You can also use this recipe as a template for substituting any omelet or quiche ingredients you most like.

Nutrition per serving: 252 calories, 10.2g fat (sat 4.4g), 69.3mg cholesterol, 35g protein, 4.3g total carbohydrate (0.8g fiber, 1.2g sugar), 1549mg sodium

# Low Calorie Instant Pot Soup and Stew Recipes

# Creamy Cauliflower and Sage Soup

Kid-Friendly
7 Ingredients or Less
20 Minutes or Less

Serves 4
Prep Time: 10 minutes
Cook Time: 10 minutes

**Ingredients**
1 teaspoon butter
1 large onion, chopped
4 cloves garlic, minced
1 teaspoon ground sage
8 cups cauliflower florets
3 cups low-sodium chicken broth
½ teaspoon salt
Pepper to taste
½ cup unsweetened coconut milk

**Directions**
Select the Sauté setting and heat the butter. Add the onion and cook until translucent, about 3-5 minutes. Add the garlic and sage and cook for 1 minute. Add the cauliflower, chicken broth, salt, and pepper, and stir well.

Press Cancel to reset the cooking method. Lock the lid and set the Pressure Release to Sealing. Select the Pressure Cook or Manual setting and set the cooking time to 10 minutes at high pressure.

Once the timer goes off, let sit for at least 10 minutes; the pressure will release naturally. Then switch the Pressure Release to Venting to allow any last steam out.

Open the Instant Pot and puree the soup using an immersion blender or by transferring it to a stand blender. Stir in the unsweetened coconut milk and add salt and pepper to taste.

Nutrition per serving:  171 calories, 9.2g fat (sat 6.9g), 5mg cholesterol, 8.8g protein, 18.1g total carbohydrate (5.8g fiber, 6.7g sugar), 411mg sodium

# Curried Pumpkin Soup

Kid-Friendly
20 Minutes or Less

Serves 4
Prep Time: 10 minutes
Cook Time: 5 minutes

2 tablespoons butter
1 onion, chopped
2 tablespoons curry powder
1/8 teaspoon cayenne pepper (optional)
4 cups vegetable broth
4 cups low-sodium pumpkin puree
1 tablespoon tamari
Salt to taste
Pepper to taste
1½ cups unsweetened coconut milk
1 teaspoon lemon juice
Optional: ¼ cup roasted pumpkin seeds for serving

**Directions**
Select the Sauté setting on the Instant Pot and heat the butter. Add the onion and cook until translucent, 3-4 minutes.

Add the curry powder and cayenne (if using), and stir until fragrant 1-2 minutes. Add the vegetable broth and 1 cup of water. Stir in the pumpkin puree and tamari. Season to taste with salt and pepper.

Press Cancel to reset the cooking method. Lock the lid and set the Pressure Release to Sealing. Select the Pressure Cook or Manual setting and set the cooking time to 5 minutes at high pressure.

Once the timer goes off, let sit for at least 10 minutes; the pressure will release naturally. Then switch the Pressure Release to Venting to allow any last steam out.

Open the Instant Pot and puree the soup using an immersion blender or by transferring it to a stand blender. Stir in the unsweetened coconut milk and add salt and pepper to taste.

Ladle into bowls and top with roasted pumpkin seeds, if desired.

Nutrition per serving:  340 calories, 24.9g fat (sat 20.1g), 15.1mg cholesterol, 5.8g protein, 30.9g total carbohydrate (8.8g fiber, 11.9g sugar), 1509mg sodium (based on .13 teaspoon of salt/serving)

# My Signature Lemon Chicken Soup

Kid-Friendly

Serves 4
Prep Time: 10 minutes
Cook Time: 6 minutes

## Ingredients
1 tablespoon olive oil
1 medium onion, chopped
3 cloves garlic, roughly chopped
2 medium carrots, peeled and sliced
6 stalks celery, sliced
8 cups fat-free chicken broth
1 teaspoon dried thyme
Salt to taste
Pepper to taste
1½ lbs. boneless skinless chicken breasts
4 oz. whole wheat spaghetti, broken in 1-inch pieces
1 bunch kale, stemmed and roughly chopped, to yield 1.5 cups
2 lemons, juiced
Optional: lemon wedges for serving

## Directions
Select the Sauté setting and heat the olive oil. Add the onion, garlic, carrots, and celery and sauté for 4-6 minutes. Add the chicken broth and thyme. Taste and add salt and pepper to taste. Add the chicken breasts and stir well.

Press Cancel to reset the cooking method. Lock the lid and set the Pressure Release to Sealing. Select the Soup setting and set the cooking time to 6 minutes at high pressure.

Once the timer goes off, let sit for at least 10 minutes; the pressure will release naturally. Then switch the Pressure Release to Venting to allow any last steam out.

Open the Instant Pot and remove the chicken and shred. Add the broken spaghetti and stir; cook for time indicated on package. Add the chicken back to the pot and stir in the kale and lemon juice. Ladle into bowls and serve with an extra squeeze of lemon, drizzle of olive oil, or fresh cracked pepper.

Nutrition per serving:  388 calories, 7g fat (sat 1.2g), 97.4mg cholesterol, 45g protein, 35.1g total carbohydrate (3.0g fiber, 5.0g sugar), 2318mg sodium (based on .13 teaspoon salt/serving)

# Fuss-Free French Onion Soup

7 Ingredients or Less

Serves 4
Prep Time: 5 minutes
Cook Time: 20 minutes

**Ingredients**
3 tablespoons unsalted butter
3 large yellow onions, halved and then thinly sliced
2 tablespoons balsamic vinegar
6 cups beef broth
2 large sprigs fresh thyme
1 teaspoon salt

**Directions**
Select the Sauté setting and heat the butter. Add the onions and stir constantly until completely cooked down and caramelized. This can take 20-30 minutes or more, depending on your onions and the heat of your Instant Pot. You're looking for a deep caramel color. If the onions begin to blacken at the edges, use the Adjust button to reduce the heat to Less.

Once the onions have caramelized, add the balsamic vinegar, red wine vinegar, broth, thyme, and salt, and scrape up any browned bits from the bottom of the pot.

Press Cancel to reset the cooking method. Lock the lid and set the Pressure Release to Sealing. Select the Soup setting and set the cooking time to 10 minutes at high pressure.

Once the timer goes off, let sit for at least 10 minutes; the pressure will release naturally. Then switch the Pressure Release to Venting to allow any last steam out.

Open the Instant Pot and discard the thyme stems. Season with salt and pepper to taste and serve warm.

Nutrition per serving:  151 calories, 9.4g fat (sat 5.8g), 22.6mg cholesterol, 5.5g protein, 11.5g total carbohydrate (2g fiber, 5.4g sugar), 1762mg sodium

# Creamy Broccoli and Apple Soup

Kid-Friendly
20 Minutes or Less

Serves 4
Prep Time: 5 minutes
Cook Time: 5 minutes

**Ingredients**
2 tablespoons butter
3 medium leeks, white parts only (frozen is fine!)
2 shallots, chopped, about 3 tablespoons
1 large head broccoli, cut into florets
1 large apple, peeled, cored, and diced
4 cups vegetable broth
1 cup unsweetened coconut milk
Pepper to taste
Salt to taste
Optional: ¼ cup walnuts, toasted
Optional: ¼ cup coconut cream

**Directions**
Select the Sauté setting and heat the butter. Add the leeks and shallots and cook, stirring constantly, until softened, 4-6 minutes. Add the broccoli and apple and sauté another 5-6 minutes. Add the vegetable broth and stir well.

Press Cancel to reset the cooking method. Lock the lid and set the Pressure Release to Sealing. Select the Pressure Cook or Manual setting and set the cooking time to 5 minutes at high pressure.

Once the timer goes off, let sit for at least 10 minutes; the pressure will release naturally. Then switch the Pressure Release to Venting to allow any last steam out.

Open the Instant Pot and puree the soup using an immersion blender or by transferring it to a stand blender. Stir in the unsweetened coconut milk and add salt and pepper to taste.

Ladle into bowls and top with toasted walnuts or a drizzle of coconut cream.

Nutrition per serving:  259 calories, 14.3g fat (sat 11.7g), 3.8mg cholesterol, 6.8g protein, 32.3g total carbohydrate (5.9g fiber, 12.6g sugar), 1303mg sodium (based on .13 teaspoon salt/serving)

# Immune-Boost Chard and Sweet Potato Stew

20 Minutes or Less

Serves 2
Prep Time: 10 minutes
Cook Time: 8 minutes

**Ingredients**
2 tablespoons olive oil
1 teaspoon cumin seeds, or 1 teaspoon ground cumin
1 medium onion, diced
2 medium sweet potatoes, peeled and in ½ inch cubes
½ teaspoon turmeric
1 tablespoon fresh ginger, peeled and minced
1 teaspoon salt
1 teaspoon ground coriander
2 cups vegetable broth
1 bunch Swiss chard (about 12 oz)
Optional: lemon wedges for serving

**Directions**
Select the Sauté setting and heat the olive oil. Add the onion and cook until translucent, 3-5 minutes. If using cumin seeds, add them now and toast them for 1-3 minutes, until fragrant. Otherwise, add the ground cumin in the next step.

Add the sweet potato, ground cumin (if using), ginger, turmeric, coriander, and salt and cook for 3-4 minutes. Add the vegetable broth and chard. Taste and add more salt and pepper if needed.

Press Cancel to reset the cooking method. Lock the lid and set the Pressure Release to Sealing. Select the Pressure Cook or Manual setting and set the cooking time to 8 minutes at high pressure.

Once the timer goes off, let sit for at least 10 minutes; the pressure will release naturally. Then switch the Pressure Release to Venting to allow any last steam out.

Ladle into bowls and serve warm with a squeeze of lemon juice, if desired.

Nutrition per serving:  308 calories, 14.4g fat (sat 2g), 0mg cholesterol, 6.2g protein, 42.6g total carbohydrate (8.3g fiber, 11.8g sugar), 2552mg sodium

# Moroccan Lentil Soup

Kid-Friendly
20 Minutes or Less

Serves 4
Prep Time: 10 minutes
Cook Time: 10 minutes

**Ingredients**
1 tablespoon olive oil
1 small onion, chopped
3 cloves garlic, minced
3/4 lb. ground turkey
1 tablespoon cumin
1 teaspoon garlic powder
1 teaspoon chili powder
1 teaspoon salt, plus more to taste
¼ teaspoon cinnamon
Pepper to taste
5 cups beef broth
1 cup green or brown lentils

**Directions**
Select the Sauté setting and heat the olive oil. Add the onion and garlic and sauté until fragrant, 2-3 minutes. Add the ground beef and cumin, garlic powder, chili powder, salt, cinnamon, and pepper. Cook until very well-browned and beginning to sear. Add the beef broth and scrape up any browned bits from the bottom of the pot. Add the lentils and stir well.

Press Cancel to reset the cooking method. Lock the lid and set the Pressure Release to Sealing. Select the Soup setting and set the cooking time to 10 minutes at high pressure.

Once the timer goes off, let sit for at least 10 minutes; the pressure will release naturally. Then switch the Pressure Release to Venting to allow any last steam out.

Open the Instant Pot and taste; add more salt and pepper to taste. Ladle into bowls and serve with a drizzle of olive oil or fresh cracked pepper.

Nutrition per serving: 364 calories, 12g fat (sat 2.8g), 67.2mg cholesterol, 31.3g protein, 32.2g total carbohydrate (15.5g fiber, 2g sugar), 1652mg sodium

# Low Calorie Instant Pot Chicken Recipes

# One-Pot Thyme Chicken and Sweet Potatoes

Kid-Friendly
20 Minutes or Less

Serves 4
Prep Time: 10 minutes
Cook Time: 10 minutes

**Ingredients**
1 ½ lbs. boneless skinless chicken breasts
1 teaspoon salt, divided
1 tablespoon olive oil
1 cup low-sodium chicken broth
2 cloves garlic, minced
1 medium onion, sliced
2 cups carrots, diced
3 medium sweet potatoes (about 1 lb. total), cut in 1-inch pieces
1 sprig fresh rosemary, or 1 teaspoon dried rosemary
1 sprig fresh thyme, or 1 teaspoon dried thyme
Pepper to taste

**Directions**
Season the chicken breasts on both sides with ½ teaspoon salt. Select the Sauté setting on the Instant Pot and heat the olive oil. Brown the chicken, about 5 minutes per side.

Add the chicken broth and scraping up any browned bits from the bottom of the pot. Layer in the garlic and onion, top with carrots, and then sweet potatoes. Sprinkle the sweet potatoes with rosemary, thyme, and the remaining ½ teaspoon of salt.

Press Cancel to reset the cooking method. Lock the lid and set the Pressure Release to Sealing. Select the Poultry setting and set the cooking time to 10 minutes.

Once the timer goes off, let sit for at least 10 minutes; the pressure will release naturally. Then switch the Pressure Release to Venting to allow any last steam out.

Open the lid, and add salt and pepper to taste. Serve in bowls with the broth.

Nutrition per serving:  349 calories, 6.1g fat (sat 1.2g), 97.4mg cholesterol, 42.6g protein, 29.9g total carbohydrate (5.4g fiber, 8.4g sugar), 862mg sodium

# Game-Time Buffalo Wings and Cauliflower Mash

Kid-Friendly
20 Minutes or Less
7 Ingredients or Less

Serves 4
Prep Time: 1 minute
Cook Time: 5 minutes

**Ingredients**
½ cup Frank's Red Hot Sauce, divided
1 teaspoon unsalted butter, melted
1.5 lbs. chicken wings
2 cups cauliflower florets

**Directions**

Add 1 cup of water to the Instant Pot and place the trivet in the pot. Toss wings and cauliflower in ¼ cup Frank's Red Hot Sauce. Arrange the chicken wings on top of the trivet, then arrange the cauliflower on top of the chicken wings. Be sure you can easily close the lid.

Lock the lid and set the Pressure Release to Sealing. Select the Pressure Cook or Manual setting and set the cooking time to 3 minutes at high pressure.

Meanwhile, in a small bowl, combine the remaining ¼ cup hot sauce and butter. Set aside.

Once the timer goes off, let sit for 5 minutes, then switch the Pressure Release to Venting to allow any last steam out.

Remove the wings to a plate and strain the remaining liquid. Mash the cauliflower. Toss the wings in the buffalo sauce and serve warm.

**Optional:** For crispier wings, spread on a foil-covered baking sheet and set under the broiler until they reach your desired level of crispiness.

Nutrition per serving:  400 calories, 27.8g fat (sat 8.1g), 132mg cholesterol, 31.8g protein, 2.7g total carbohydrate (1.3g fiber, 1.2g sugar), 1,143.5mg sodium

# Fiesta Pulled Chicken Taco Bar

Kid-Friendly
7 Ingredients or Less
20 Minutes or Less

Serves 4
Prep Time: 5 minutes
Cook Time: 7-10 minutes

**Ingredients**
2 pounds of boneless skinless chicken breast
1 tablespoon chili powder
½ tablespoon ground cumin
1 teaspoon garlic powder
1 teaspoon oregano
½ teaspoon salt
1 tablespoon olive oil
1 cup low-sodium chicken broth
1 head butter lettuce, separated into lettuce cups
Optional: guacamole, green onions, black olives, or any other favorite taco toppings

**Directions**
Season chicken on both sides with chili powder, cumin, garlic powder, oregano, and salt. Select the Sauté setting on the Instant Pot and heat the olive oil. Brown the chicken, about 5 minutes per side. Add the chicken broth and scraping up any browned bits from the bottom of the pot.

Press Cancel to reset the cooking method. Lock the lid and set the Pressure Release to Sealing. Select the Poultry setting and set the cooking time to 7 minutes for breasts and 10 minutes for thighs at high pressure.

Once the timer goes off, let sit for at least 10 minutes; the pressure will release naturally. Then switch the Pressure Release to Venting to allow any last steam out.

Open the lid and taste, adding more salt and pepper if necessary. Shred the chicken, and allow each person to assemble their own lettuce tacos or corn tortilla tacos.

**Note:** For a thicker sauce, remove 1 tablespoon of sauce to a small bowl. Dissolve 1 teaspoon arrowroot powder in the sauce, then add back to the Instant Pot and whisk well. Select the Sauté setting and allow to cook for a few minutes, whisking often, until thickened.

Nutrition per serving:  303 calories, 7.1g fat (sat 1.4g), 130mg cholesterol, 54g protein, 3.6g total carbohydrate (1.3g fiber, 0.8g sugar), 477mg sodium

# Chicken Marsala with Spaghetti Squash

Kid-Friendly

Serves 5
Prep Time: 10 minutes
Cook Time: 30 minutes

1 large spaghetti squash (about 5 lbs.)
2 lbs. boneless skinless chicken breast
1 teaspoon salt
Pepper to taste
1 teaspoon olive oil
2 cloves garlic, minced
¼ cup marsala wine
1 cup sliced white mushrooms
½ cup low-sodium chicken broth
Optional: fresh basil for serving

Place the trivet inside the Instant Pot, add 1 cup water, and place the spaghetti squash on the trivet. Lock the lid and set the Pressure Release to Sealing. Select the Manual or Pressure Cook setting and set the timer to 20 minutes at high pressure. Once the timer goes off, let sit for at least 10 minutes; the pressure will release naturally. Then switch the Pressure Release to Venting to allow any last steam out. Remove the spaghetti squash and set aside to cool.

Discard the water, dry the pot, and select the Sauté setting. Heat the olive oil, then add the chicken, salt, and pepper to taste. Sear the chicken until browned, about 5 minutes on each side. Add the garlic, marsala wine or vinegar, mushrooms, and broth, and stir to combine, scraping up any browned bits from the bottom of the pan.

Lock the lid and set the Pressure Release to Sealing. Select the Poultry setting and set the cooking time to 7 minutes at high pressure.

Meanwhile, slice the spaghetti squash in half, scoop out the seeds, and separate the squash from the rind. Once the Instant Pot timer goes off, use a kitchen towel or oven mitts to protect your hand and move the Pressure Release knob to Venting to perform a quick pressure release.

Open the lid and taste, adding more salt and pepper if necessary. Serve the chicken over the spaghetti squash noodles and top with the marsala sauce, mushrooms, and fresh basil, if desired

**Note:** For a thicker sauce, remove ¼ cup sauce. Dissolve 1 teaspoon all-purpose flour in the sauce, then add back to the pot and mix well. Allow to cook for a few minutes, until thickened.

Nutrition per serving: 375 calories, 6g fat (sat 1.3g), 104mg cholesterol, 45.7g protein, 34g total carbohydrate (0.2g fiber, 1.2g sugar), 674mg sodium

# Lemon Pepper Chicken with Cauliflower Mash

Kid-Friendly
7 Ingredients or Less
20 Minutes or Less

Serves 4
Prep Time: 15 minutes
Cook Time: 15 minutes

3 lemons, zested and juiced
1 teaspoon garlic powder
1½ teaspoons black pepper
1 teaspoon salt
2 tablespoons unsalted butter, divided
2 lbs. bone-in skinless chicken thighs
1 cup low-sodium chicken broth
4 cups cauliflower, in large florets

**Directions**
In a small bowl, combine the lemon zest, garlic powder, pepper, and salt.

Select the Sauté setting and heat 1 tablespoon of the butter. Season the chicken thighs on both sides with the lemon pepper rub. Add the chicken thighs to the pot and brown well on each side, about 4 minutes per side. You may need to work in batches.

Add chicken broth and scrape up any browned bits from the bottom. Place the trivet on top of the chicken and layer the cauliflower florets on top. Season cauliflower with salt and pepper.

Press Cancel to reset the cooking method. Lock the lid and set the Pressure Release to Sealing. Select the Poultry setting and set the cooking time to 15 minutes at high pressure.

Once the timer goes off, use a kitchen towel or oven mitts to protect your hand and move the Pressure Release knob to Venting to perform a quick pressure release.

Open the lid, remove the cauliflower to a bowl, and mash with the remaining 1 tablespoon butter and salt and pepper to taste. Serve the chicken with the cauliflower mash and drizzle the chicken with as much lemon juice as desired before serving.

**Note:** For a thicker sauce, remove 1 tablespoon of sauce to a small bowl. Dissolve 1 teaspoon all-purpose flour in the sauce, then add back to the Instant Pot and whisk well. Select the Sauté setting and allow to cook for a few minutes, whisking often, until thickened.

Nutrition per serving:  305 calories, 13g fat (sat 5.4g), 155mg cholesterol, 37.4g protein, 15.7g total carbohydrate (6.6g fiber, 2.7g sugar), 778mg sodium

# Our Go-To BBQ Drumsticks

Kid-Friendly
20 Minutes or Less
7 Ingredients or Less

Serves 4
Prep Time: 10 minutes
Cook Time: 20 minutes

**Ingredients**
¾ cup ketchup
1 tablespoon apple cider vinegar
2 tablespoons honey
1 teaspoon garlic powder
1 teaspoon paprika
¼ teaspoon cayenne pepper (Or ½ teaspoon, if you like spicy BBQ sauce.)
½ teaspoon salt
Optional: 1 teaspoon liquid smoke
8 chicken drumsticks

**Directions**
Select the Sauté setting on the Instant Pot. Add all of the ingredients except the drumsticks and stir well. Allow to cook for at least 10 minutes, until thickened. Taste and adjust salt or spice level to your taste.

Ladle the sauce out of the Instant Pot, but no need to wipe it clean. Add 1 cup of water to the pot and place the trivet in the bottom of the pot. Arrange the drumsticks on top of the trivet.

Lock the lid and set the Pressure Release to Sealing. Select the Poultry setting and set the cooking time to 20 minutes at high pressure.

Once the timer goes off and with a kitchen towel or oven mitts protecting your hand, move the Pressure Release knob to Venting to perform a quick pressure release. Toss the drumsticks in the BBQ sauce and serve warm.

**Optional:** For crispier, more charred drumsticks, spread the drumsticks on a baking sheet and set under the broiler until they reach your desired level of char.

Nutrition per serving:  315 calories, 12.9g fat (sat 3.5g), 118mg cholesterol, 29.2g protein, 20.8g total carbohydrate (0.4g fiber, 19.1g sugar), 630.5mg sodium

# Creamy Chicken and Broccoli Shells

Kid-Friendly
7 ingredients or Less

Prep time: 10 minutes
Cook time: 15 minutes

Serves 4

2 teaspoons olive oil
¾ lb. boneless skinless chicken breasts, in 1-inch cubes
1 teaspoon salt
6 garlic cloves, chopped
8 oz. whole wheat pasta shells, uncooked
3 cups fat-free chicken broth
6 cups broccoli florets
¼ cup parmesan cheese
Freshly ground pepper to taste

Select the Sauté setting on the Instant Pot and heat the olive oil. Add the chicken, season with the salt and pepper, and cook until browned, 5-7 minutes. Add the garlic and cook for 1 minute more, until fragrant.

Add the chicken broth and scrape up any browned bits at the bottom of the pot. Arrange the chicken in an even layer and add the shells on top. Press shells down until mostly submerged, then layer the broccoli on top.

Lock the lid and set the Pressure Release to Sealing. Select the Manual setting and set the cooking time to 3 minutes at high pressure. Once the Instant Pot timer goes off, use a kitchen towel or oven mitts to protect your hand and move the Pressure Release knob to Venting to perform a quick pressure release.

Press Cancel to reset the cooking method and select the Sauté setting. Open the pot and add parmesan cheese and more salt and pepper to taste. Stir well, mashing broccoli and adding more broth if needed to form a pesto-like sauce. Serve warm, with a drizzle of olive oil and more parmesan cheese, if desired.

Nutrition per serving: 394 calories, 6.7g fat (sat 1.9g), 54.2mg cholesterol, 35g protein, 53.1g total carbohydrate (8.3g fiber, 2.7g sugar), 1478mg sodium

# Better-Than-Store-Bought Rotisserie Chicken

Kid-Friendly
7 Ingredients or Less

Serves 6
Prep Time: 15 minutes
Cook Time: 20 minutes

**Ingredients**
1 4-lb. whole chicken
2 tablespoons olive oil
1 lemon, juiced and zested
1 tablespoon garlic powder
2 teaspoons dried thyme
2 teaspoons salt
¼ teaspoon pepper
1 cup low-sodium chicken broth

**Directions**
Pat the chicken dry with paper towels. In a small bowl, mix olive oil, lemon zest, garlic powder, thyme, salt, and pepper, and rub the chicken with the herb oil.

Select the Sauté setting and add the chicken, back side down, to the pot. Sear for 6-7 minutes, until well browned, then flip and brown the breast side for another 6-7 minutes. Add the chicken broth and scrape up any browned bits stuck to the bottom of the pot.

Press Cancel to reset the cooking method. Lock the lid and set the Pressure Release to Sealing. Select the Poultry setting and set the cooking time to 20 minutes at high pressure.

Once the timer goes off, use a kitchen towel or oven mitts to protect your hand and move the Pressure Release knob to Venting to perform a quick pressure release.

Open the lid, and taste, adding more salt and pepper to the sauce if necessary. Transfer to a platter, carve, and serve warm, drizzled with the lemon juice.

**Note:** For a thicker sauce, remove 1 tablespoon of sauce to a small bowl. Dissolve 1 teaspoon all-purpose flour in the sauce, then add back to the Instant Pot and whisk well. Select the Sauté setting and allow to cook for a few minutes, whisking often, until thickened.

Nutrition per serving:  367 calories, 23.6g fat (sat 5.9g), 106mg cholesterol, 34.7g protein, 3.7g total carbohydrate (1g fiber, 0.3g sugar), 988mg sodium

# Italian White Bean and Chicken Bowls

Kid-Friendly

Serves 4
Prep Time: 5 minutes
Cook Time: 40 minutes

**Ingredients**
1 ¼ cup dried white beans, such as great northern, cannellini, or chickpeas
1 small onion, chopped
3 cloves garlic, minced
½ teaspoon dried thyme
½ teaspoon dried oregano
1 teaspoon salt
Pepper to taste
3½ cups low-sodium chicken broth
1 lb. boneless chicken breasts, cut in 2-inch pieces
2 cups broccoli florets
1 lemon, juiced
Optional: Replace the thyme and oregano with 1 teaspoon of Italian Seasoning (recipe found in the Seasonings chapter).

**Directions**
In the Instant Pot, add the beans, onion, garlic, thyme, oregano, salt, pepper, and broth. Stir well and spread out the beans so that they're in an even layer and submerged in the broth. Place the chicken in an even layer over the beans.

Lock the lid and set the Pressure Release to Sealing. Select the Pressure Cook or Manual setting and set the cooking time to 40 minutes at high pressure.

Once the timer goes off, let sit for at least 10 minutes; the pressure will release naturally. Then switch the Pressure Release to Venting to allow any last steam out.

Open the Instant Pot and taste, adding more salt and pepper if needed. Select the Sauté setting and add the broccoli; allow to cook for 3-5 minutes, until tender. Spoon into bowls and serve warm, drizzled with the lemon juice.

Nutrition per serving: 381 calories, 3.5g fat (sat 1.0g), 65mg cholesterol, 44.3g protein, 44.8g total carbohydrate (13.3g fiber, 3.4g sugar), 742mg sodium

# Low Calorie Instant Pot Seafood Recipes

# Better-Than-Takeout Asian Salmon with Broccoli

Kid-Friendly
20 Minutes or Less

Serves 4
Prep Time: 5 minutes
Cook Time: 3 minutes

**Ingredients:**
2 cloves garlic, minced
¼ teaspoon crushed red pepper
½ teaspoon salt
Pepper to taste
3 tablespoons soy sauce
1 cup low-sodium chicken broth
2 cups broccoli florets
4 medium-sized salmon fillets (about 5 ½ oz. each)
½ lime, juiced
1 tablespoon sesame oil

**Directions**
In a small bowl, combine half of the minced garlic, crushed red pepper, salt, pepper, and 2 tablespoons of the soy sauce. Brush the sauce on the salmon fillets.

In the Instant Pot, add 1 cup of chicken broth and place the trivet in the bottom of the pot. Add the broccoli florets, and season to taste with salt and pepper. Arrange the salmon fillets on top of the broccoli.

Lock the lid and set the Pressure Release to Sealing. Select the Steam setting and set the cooking time to 2 minutes. Meanwhile, in a small bowl, combine the lime juice, remaining minced garlic, remaining 1 tablespoon of soy sauce, sesame oil, and salt and pepper to taste.

With a kitchen towel or oven mitts protecting your hand, move the Pressure Release knob to Venting to perform a quick pressure release.

Open the lid and taste, adding more salt and pepper if necessary. Serve the salmon and broccoli with the sesame oil sauce. This is also great served over a bowl of white sticky rice.

Nutrition per serving:  317 calories, 16.1g fat (sat 3.5g), 81.1mg cholesterol, 37.7g protein, 4.8g total carbohydrate (0.4g fiber, 0.5g sugar), 1148mg sodium

# Easy Lemon Garlic Salmon with Cauliflower

Kid-Friendly
20 Minutes or Less
7 Ingredients or Less

Serves 4
Prep Time: 5 minutes
Cook Time: 3 minutes

**Ingredients:**
4 cloves garlic, minced
1 teaspoon salt, divided
Pepper to taste
2 tablespoons unsalted butter, divided
2 tablespoons lemon juice, divided
1 medium onion, sliced
3 cups cauliflower in small florets
4 medium-sized salmon fillets, (about 5 ½ oz. each)

**Directions**
In a small bowl, combine half of the minced garlic, ½ teaspoon salt, pepper, and 1 tablespoon each of the butter and lemon juice. Brush the lemon garlic sauce on the salmon fillets.

In the Instant Pot, add 1 cup of chicken broth and place the trivet in the bottom of the pot. Add the onions and cauliflower, and season lightly with salt and pepper. Arrange the salmon fillets on top of the onions and cauliflower.

Lock the lid and set the Pressure Release to Sealing. Select the Steam setting and set the cooking time to 3 minutes at high pressure. Meanwhile, in a small bowl, combine the remaining minced garlic, remaining 1 tablespoon of butter, lemon juice, and salt and pepper to taste.

Once the timer has gone off and with a kitchen towel or oven mitts protecting your hand, move the Pressure Release knob to Venting to perform a quick pressure release.

Open the lid and taste, adding more salt and pepper if necessary. Serve the salmon and cauliflower with the lemon garlic sauce.

Nutrition per serving:  341 calories, 18g fat (sat 6.5g), 96.2mg cholesterol, 35.9g protein, 8.2g total carbohydrate (2.4g fiber, 3.2g sugar), 681mg sodium

# Light and Fresh Mediterranean Cod

20 Minutes or Less

Serves 6
Prep Time: 10 minutes
Cook Time: 6 minutes

**Ingredients**
1 tablespoon butter
1 lemon, juiced
1 medium onion, sliced
½ teaspoon salt
½ teaspoon black pepper
1 teaspoon dried oregano
1-28 oz. can white beans
1 cup low-sodium chicken broth
2 tablespoons capers, drained,
6 cod fillets, about 8 oz. each

**Directions**
Select the Sauté setting and heat the butter. Add the remaining ingredients, except for the cod. Cook the sauce for 10 minutes. Place the cod fillets in the sauce and spoon sauce over each fillet.

Press Cancel to reset the cooking method. Lock the lid and set the Pressure Release to Sealing. Select the Steam setting and set the cooking time to 3 minutes at high pressure.

Once the timer has gone off and with a kitchen towel or oven mitts protecting your hand, move the Pressure Release knob to Venting to perform a quick pressure release.

Open the lid and taste the sauce, adding more salt and pepper if necessary. Serve the cod with the beans and Mediterranean sauce.

Nutrition per serving: 372 calories, 4.1g fat (sat 1.7g), 104mg cholesterol, 51.8g protein, 30.9g total carbohydrate (6.8g fiber, 1.4g sugar), 422mg sodium

# 5-Minute Citrus Shrimp

Kid-Friendly
20 Minutes or Less
7 Ingredients or Less

Serves 4
Prep Time: 5 minutes
Cook Time: 1 minute

**Ingredients**
1 tablespoon butter
4 garlic cloves, minced
½ cup orange juice (100% pure, no sugar added)
½ cup low-sodium chicken broth
2 pounds of peeled and deveined raw shrimp
2 tablespoons lemon juice
1 teaspoon salt
Pepper to taste

**Directions**
Select the Sauté setting and heat the butter. Add the garlic and cook until fragrant, 1-2 minutes. Add the orange juice and chicken broth.

Press Cancel to reset the cooking method, add the shrimp, and season with ½ teaspoon salt. Lock the lid and set the Pressure Release to Sealing. Select the Steam setting and set the cooking time to 1 minute at high pressure.

Once the timer has gone off and with a kitchen towel or oven mitts protecting your hand, move the Pressure Release knob to Venting to perform a quick pressure release.

Open the lid and stir in lemon juice and adjust salt and pepper to taste. Serve over white or brown rice, cauliflower rice, or mixed vegetables.

Nutrition per serving:  288 calories, 7g fat (sat 2.6g), 348mg cholesterol, 46.6g protein, 7.3g total carbohydrate (0.2g fiber, 2.9g sugar), 922mg sodium

# Low Calorie Instant Pot Pork Recipes

# Sunday Favorite Pork Ragu

Kid-Friendly
7 Ingredients or Less

Serves 4
Prep Time: 5 minutes
Cook Time: 45 minutes

**Ingredients**
18 oz. pork tenderloin
1 teaspoon salt
Pepper to taste
1 tablespoon olive oil
6 garlic cloves
1-28 oz. can crushed tomatoes, with juices
2 teaspoons dried thyme
1 teaspoon dried oregano
Optional: 2 bay leaves

**Directions**
Season the pork loin with salt and pepper. Select the Sauté setting on the Instant Pot and heat the olive oil. Add the pork loin to the Instant Pot and sear on all sides until browned. Add the garlic, crushed tomatoes, thyme, oregano, and if using, bay leaves.

Lock the lid and set the Pressure Release to Sealing. Select the Meat/Stew setting and set the cooking time to 45 minutes at high pressure.

Once the timer goes off, let sit for at least 10 minutes; the pressure will release naturally. Then switch the Pressure Release to Venting to allow any last steam out.

Open the lid and taste, adding more salt and pepper if necessary. Shred the pork and serve over your favorite low-carb pasta, spaghetti squash, or spooned over vegetable fritters.

Nutrition per serving:  223 calories, 8.2g fat (sat 2g), 81.9mg cholesterol, 27.9g protein, 9.8g total carbohydrate (2.3g fiber, 4.7g sugar), 928mg sodium

# Mushroom Smothered Pork Chops

7 Ingredients or Less
20 Minutes or Less

Serves 4
Prep Time: 10 minutes
Cook Time: 15 minutes

**Ingredients**
4 ½-inch thick bone-in pork chops (about 5 oz. each)
½ teaspoon paprika
½ teaspoon garlic powder
1 teaspoon salt
½ teaspoon ground black pepper
1 tablespoon unsalted butter
1 medium onion, sliced
6 oz. white mushrooms
½ cup low-sodium chicken broth
Optional: 1 teaspoon all-purpose flour

**Directions**
Season the pork chops with paprika, garlic powder, salt and pepper. Select the Sauté setting on the Instant Pot and heat the butter. Brown the chops on both sides then remove to a plate, working in batches of 2 chops at a time if necessary. Set aside the browned chops.

Add the onion and mushrooms and cook for about 3 minutes, stirring well. Add the chicken broth and nestle the pork chops back into the sauce.

Press Cancel to reset the cooking method. Lock the lid and set the Pressure Release to Sealing. Select the Meat/Stew setting and set the cooking time to 15 minutes at high pressure.

Once the timer has gone off and with a kitchen towel or oven mitts protecting your hand, move the Pressure Release knob to Venting to perform a quick pressure release.

Open the lid and taste, adding more salt and pepper if necessary. Remove the pork chops to a platter and allow to rest for 2-3 minutes before serving drizzled with the mushroom sauce. Serve with your favorite low-carb pasta or a baked potato.

**Note:** For a thicker sauce, remove 1 tablespoon of sauce to a small bowl. Dissolve 1 teaspoon all-purpose flour in the sauce, then add back to the Instant Pot and whisk well. Select the Sauté setting and allow to cook for a few minutes, whisking often, until thickened.

Nutrition per serving: 366 calories, 29.8g fat (sat 11.1g), 86.7mg cholesterol, 19.8g protein, 4.9g total carbohydrate (1.1g fiber, 2g sugar), 654mg sodium

# Artichoke and Lemon Pork Chops

Kid-Friendly
20 Minutes or Less

Serves 4
Prep Time: 10 minutes
Cook Time: 15 minutes

## Ingredients
3 oz. bacon, diced (about 3 slices)
4 ½-inch thick bone-in pork chops, fat trimmed (about 5 oz. each)
1/2 teaspoon ground black pepper
1 shallot, minced
1 teaspoon lemon zest
3 garlic cloves, minced
1 teaspoon dried rosemary
1 cup low-sodium chicken broth
1 9-oz package frozen artichoke heart quarters

## Directions
Select the Sauté setting and add the bacon. Cook until it has rendered its fat and turned crispy, about 5 minutes. Transfer the bacon to a plate.

Season the pork chops with salt and pepper and add to the Instant Pot. Brown the chops on both sides then remove to a plate, working in batches of 2 chops at a time if necessary.

Add shallots to the pot and cook for 1 minute. Add lemon zest, garlic, and rosemary and cook until fragrant. Add the chicken broth, artichokes, and cooked bacon. Stir well then nestle the chops back into the sauce.

Press Cancel to reset the cooking method. Lock the lid and set the Pressure Release to Sealing. Select the Meat/Stew setting and set the cooking time to 15 minutes at high pressure.

Once the timer has gone off and with a kitchen towel or oven mitts protecting your hand, move the Pressure Release knob to Venting to perform a quick pressure release.

Open the lid and taste, adding salt and pepper if necessary. Serve the pork chops with the lemon artichoke sauce.

Nutrition per serving: 318 calories, 15.4g fat (sat 4.9g), 111mg cholesterol, 36.5g protein, 8.1g total carbohydrate (2.8g fiber, 0.1g sugar), 306mg sodium

# Cuban Pulled Pork

Kid-Friendly
7 Ingredients or Less

Serve: 6
Prep Time: 5 minutes
Cook Time: 80 minutes

## Ingredients
3 lbs. boneless pork shoulder, fat trimmed
6 cloves garlic
½ cup grapefruit juice
½ cup fat-free chicken broth
1 teaspoon dried oregano
1 tablespoon cumin
1 lime, juiced
2 teaspoons salt
1 bay leaf
Optional for serving: lime wedges, cilantro, salsa, or hot sauce

## Directions
Cut the pork shoulder into 4 evenly sized pieces. In a blender or food processor, combine the garlic, grapefruit juice, chicken broth, oregano, cumin, lime juice, and salt, and blend until combined. Place the pork shoulder pieces in the Instant Pot and rub with the sauce.

Lock the lid and set the Pressure Release to Sealing. Select the Meat/Stew setting and set the cooking time to 80 minutes at high pressure.

Once the timer goes off, let sit for at least 10 minutes; the pressure will release naturally. Then switch the Pressure Release to Venting to allow any last steam out.

Open the lid and taste, adding more salt and pepper if necessary. Remove the pork, shred, ladle sauce over it, and serve warm. This pairs well with fluffy white or brown rice or roasted vegetables.

**Note:** For a thicker sauce, add the shredded pork back to the Instant Pot with the sauce. Select the Sauté setting and cook for 5-10 minutes until sauce has soaked into the pork.

Nutrition per serving:  356 calories, 16.5g fat (sat 5.6g), 152mg cholesterol, 45.1g protein, 4.1g total carbohydrate (0.3g fiber, 0.2g sugar), 1105mg sodium

# 6-Ingredient Kahlua Pork

Kid-Friendly
7 Ingredients or Less

Serves 6
Prep Time: 15 minutes
Cook Time: 80 minutes

**Ingredients**
3 lbs. boneless pork shoulder, fat trimmed
2 oz. bacon, diced (about 2 slices)
2 teaspoons salt
Pepper to taste
1 cup low-sodium chicken broth
½ cup canned diced unsweetened pineapple in juice
6 cloves garlic
1 tablespoon liquid smoke
Whole wheat dinner rolls (optional)

**Directions**
Select the Sauté setting and add the bacon. Cook until the bacon has rendered its fat and turned crispy, about 5 minutes. Transfer the bacon to a plate.

Cut the pork shoulder into 4 evenly sized pieces and season with salt and pepper. Add to the Instant Pot and sear on all sides until brown, about 4-6 minutes per side. Add 1 cup of chicken broth, diced pineapple, garlic, and liquid smoke.

Press Cancel to reset the cooking method. Lock the lid and set the Pressure Release to Sealing. Select the Meat/Stew setting and set the cooking time to 80 minutes at high pressure.

Once the timer goes off, let sit for at least 10 minutes; the pressure will release naturally. Then switch the Pressure Release to Venting to allow any last steam out.

Open the lid and taste, adding more salt and pepper if necessary. Remove the pork, shred it, ladle sauce over it, and serve warm. Or, to serve as a sandwich, tuck the pork into your favorite low-carb dinner roll and top with the sauce.

**Note:** For a thicker sauce, add the shredded pork back to the Instant Pot with the sauce. Select the Sauté setting and cook for 3-5 minutes until sauce has soaked into the pork.

Nutrition per serving: 396 calories, 20.7g fat (sat 7.1g), 158mg cholesterol, 26g protein, 3.2g total carbohydrate (0.2g fiber, 1.6g sugar), 1038mg sodium

# Balsamic Glazed Pork Tenderloin

Kid-Friendly
7 Ingredients or Less
20 Minutes or Less

Serves 4
Prep Time: 15 minutes
Cook Time: 15 minutes

## Ingredients
2 tablespoons unsalted butter
1½ lb. boneless pork tenderloin
1 teaspoon salt
½ teaspoon black pepper
1 teaspoon garlic powder
1 large red onion, thinly sliced
1/3 cup balsamic vinegar
½ cup low-sodium chicken broth
Optional: 1 teaspoon all-purpose flour

## Directions
Select the Sauté setting and heat the butter. Season the pork loin on all sides with salt, pepper, and garlic powder. Add to the Instant Pot and sear on all sides until brown, about 3-4 minutes per side. Transfer the loin to a plate and set aside.

Add red onion to the Instant Pot and cook for 3-5 minutes, until translucent. Add balsamic vinegar and chicken broth, stir well, then nestle the pork loin back into the Instant Pot.

Press Cancel to reset the cooking method. Lock the lid and set the Pressure Release to Sealing. Select the Meat/Stew setting and set the cooking time to 15 minutes at high pressure.

Once the timer goes off, let sit for at least 10 minutes; the pressure will release naturally. Then switch the Pressure Release to Venting to allow any last steam out.

Open the lid and taste, adding more salt and pepper if necessary. Transfer the pork loin to a cutting board and allow to rest for 5 minutes. Slice and serve with the balsamic glaze.

**Note:** For a thicker glaze, remove 1 tablespoon of sauce to a small bowl. Dissolve 1 teaspoon all-purpose flour in the sauce, then add back to the Instant Pot and whisk well. Select the Sauté setting and allow to cook for a few minutes, whisking often, until thickened.

Nutrition per serving:  300 calories, 11.7g fat (sat 5.6g), 124mg cholesterol, 35.8g protein, 10.4g total carbohydrate (0.9g fiber, 7.3g sugar), 683mg sodium

# Cumin-Spiced Pulled Pork Carnitas

Kid-Friendly

Serves 8
Prep Time: 7 minutes
Cook Time: 40 minutes

2 ½ lbs. boneless pork shoulder, quartered, fat trimmed
1 teaspoon olive oil
¾ cup fat-free chicken broth
1 head butter lettuce
½ small green cabbage, shredded
3 tablespoons reduced-fat mayonnaise
2 teaspoons mustard
1 tablespoon apple cider vinegar

*For spice rub:*
1 tablespoon cumin
1 tablespoon garlic powder
2 teaspoons salt
2 teaspoons oregano
½ teaspoon pepper
¼ teaspoon cayenne pepper

In a large bowl, combine the spice rub ingredients and rub on the pork shoulder pieces. Select the Sauté setting and heat the olive oil. Add the pork shoulder to the Instant Pot and sear on all sides until brown, about 3-4 minutes per side. Add ¾ cup chicken broth and scrape up any browned bits at the bottom of the pot.

Press Cancel to reset the cooking method. Lock the lid and set the Pressure Release to Sealing. Select the Meat/Stew setting and set the cooking time to 40 minutes at high pressure. Meanwhile, in a medium bowl, combine cabbage, mayonnaise, mustard, apple cider vinegar, and salt and pepper to taste. Set aside.

Once the timer goes off, let sit for at least 10 minutes; the pressure will release naturally. Then switch the Pressure Release to Venting to allow any last steam out. Remove the lid and taste the sauce; adjust seasoning if necessary. Shred the pork shoulder and serve in butter lettuce cups, topped with the cabbage slaw.

**Optional:** For a thicker sauce, add the shredded pork back to the Instant Pot with the sauce. Select the Sauté setting and cook for 5-10 minutes until sauce has soaked into the pork.

Nutrition per serving: 398 calories, 19.9g fat (sat 6.1g), 152mg cholesterol, 46.2g protein, 6.5g total carbohydrate (2.3g fiber, 2.9g sugar), 1150mg sodium

# Low-Calorie Instant Pot Beef Recipes

# Steak Fajita Stuffed Sweet Potatoes

Kid-Friendly

Serves 4
Prep Time: 15 Minutes
Cook Time: 20 minutes

2 teaspoons olive oil, divided
¾ lb. skirt steak, sliced
2 medium onions, sliced
2 medium peppers (any color), sliced
1 cup beef broth
4 medium sweet potatoes

*For fajita seasoning:*
1 tablespoon cumin
2 teaspoons chili powder
2 teaspoons garlic powder
1 teaspoon dried oregano
1 teaspoon salt
¼ teaspoon cayenne pepper, or to taste

In a small bowl, combine cumin, chili powder, garlic powder, oregano, salt, and cayenne pepper. Prick potatoes with a fork to allow steam to vent and wrap them in aluminum foil.

Select the Sauté setting on the Instant Pot and heat 1 teaspoon of the olive oil. Add half of the steak and sear on all sides. Remove to a plate and sear the second half of the steak. Remove to a plate again. Add remaining 1 teaspoon olive oil to the pot then add the onion and peppers. Stir once, allow to sear for 2-3 minutes, then stir again. Repeat until slightly charred but still firm.

Add the beef broth to the Instant Pot and scrape up any browned bits from the bottom of the pot. Add the steak and spice mix and stir well. Place the trivet over the steak and onion. Place the foil-wrapped potatoes on top of the trivet. (It's okay if they get a bit wet with sauce.)

Press Cancel to reset the cooking method. Lock the lid and set the Pressure Release to Sealing. Select the Meat/Stew setting and set the cooking time to 20 minutes at high pressure. Once the timer goes off, let sit for at least 10 minutes; the pressure will release naturally. Then switch the Pressure Release to Venting to allow any last steam out.

Remove the baked potatoes, slice open, and stuff with the steak and vegetable mix. Serve with a squeeze of lime or guacamole.

Nutrition per serving: 350 calories, 13.4g fat (sat 4.5g), 51mg cholesterol, 26.1g protein, 31.5g total carbohydrate (5.8g fiber, 7.3g sugar), 930mg sodium

# Cajun Beef and Brussels Sprout Bowls

20 Minutes or Less

Serves 4
Prep Time: 15 minutes
Cook Time: 5 minutes

**Ingredients**
2 tablespoons olive oil, divided
1½ lbs. beef stew meat (bottom round), in 1-inch cubes
1 teaspoon salt
½ teaspoon pepper
1 teaspoon garlic powder
½ teaspoon paprika
½ teaspoon chili powder
¼ teaspoon cayenne pepper
½ teaspoon dried thyme
½ teaspoon dried oregano
1½ cups beef broth
1 large onion, quartered
1 lb. brussels sprouts, halved

**Directions**
Select the Sauté setting and heat 1 tablespoon of the olive oil. Add the beef and season with salt, pepper, garlic powder, paprika, chili powder, cayenne pepper, thyme, and oregano. Sear until well-browned on all sides, 5-7 minutes.

Add the beef broth to the Instant Pot and scrape up any browned bits from the bottom of the pot. Place trivet over the beef (it's okay if it's in the broth a bit). Layer the onion and brussels sprouts on top of the trivet and season lightly with salt and pepper.

Press Cancel to reset the cooking method. Lock the lid and set the Pressure Release to Sealing. Select the Manual or Pressure Cook setting and set the cooking time to 5 minutes at high pressure.

When the timer goes off, use a kitchen towel or oven mitts to protect your hand and move the Pressure Release knob to Venting to perform a quick pressure release.

Open the lid and taste, adding more salt and pepper if necessary. Spoon the brussels sprouts and onions into individual bowls and served topped with the beef, either shredded or in chunks, and the sauce from the pot.

Nutrition per serving:  370 calories, 15.8g fat (sat 4g), 113mg cholesterol, 42.8g protein, 14.8g total carbohydrate (5.4g fiber, 4.3g sugar), 1002mg sodium

# Easiest Spaghetti with Meat Sauce

Kid-Friendly
20 Minutes or Less
7 Ingredients or Less

Serves 5
Prep Time: 1 minute
Cook Time: 10 minutes

**Directions**
1 teaspoon olive oil
¾ lb. ground turkey (93% lean)
½ small onion, diced
1 teaspoon salt
Pepper to taste
4 garlic cloves, chopped
8 oz. whole wheat spaghetti, uncooked
1 25-oz. jar of your favorite pasta sauce
2 cups fat-free chicken broth
Grated parmesan cheese (optional)

**Ingredients**
Select the Sauté setting on the Instant Pot and heat the olive oil. Add the ground turkey and onion, season with salt and pepper, and cook until well-browned, 6-8 minutes. Add the garlic and cook for 1 minute more, until fragrant.

Arrange the ground turkey in an even layer and add the spaghetti on top, broken in half so it fits in the pot. Pour in the chicken broth and pasta sauce and gently press spaghetti down into liquid until submerged.

Lock the lid and set the Pressure Release to Sealing. Select the Manual setting and set the cooking time to 7 minutes at high pressure. Once the Instant Pot timer goes off, use a kitchen towel or oven mitts to protect your hand and move the Pressure Release knob to Venting to perform a quick pressure release.

Open the pot and season with salt and pepper to taste. Stir well, adding more broth if needed. Serve warm, with a drizzle of olive oil and parmesan cheese, if desired.

Nutrition per serving: 400 calories, 11.1g fat (sat 2.8g), 56.5mg cholesterol, 21.7g protein, 54.4g total carbohydrate (3.7g fiber, 12.5g sugar), 1013mg sodium

# One-Pot Beef, Sweet Potato, and Kale Stew

Kid-Friendly

Serves 6
Prep Time: 10 minutes
Cook Time: 35 minutes

## Ingredients
1 lb. beef stew meat, (bottom round), in 1-inch cubes
1 teaspoon salt
½ teaspoon pepper
1 tablespoon olive oil
1 medium onion, chopped
1 bunch kale, stemmed and chopped (about 2 cups)
2 medium sweet potatoes, cut in 2-inch pieces
4 medium carrots, sliced (about ½ pound)
2 cups beef broth
1 tablespoon red wine vinegar
1 teaspoon paprika
1 teaspoon onion powder
Optional: 1 teaspoon arrowroot powder

## Directions
Season the meat with salt and pepper. Select the Sauté setting on the Instant Pot and heat the olive oil. Sear the meat until well-browned, 8-10 minutes. Add the onion, kale, sweet potatoes, carrots, beef broth, red wine vinegar, paprika, onion powder, and stir well.

Press Cancel to reset the cooking method. Lock the lid and set the Pressure Release to Sealing. Select the Meat/Stew setting and set the cooking time to 35 minutes at high pressure.

Once the timer goes off, let sit for at least 10 minutes; the pressure will release naturally. Then switch the Pressure Release to Venting to allow any last steam out.

Open the pot and taste the stew; adjust the seasoning if necessary.

**Optional:** For a thicker stew, ladle ¼ cup of the sauce into a small bowl and mix in 1 teaspoon arrowroot powder. Pour back into the Instant Pot, stir, and cook on the Sauté setting until thickened.

Nutrition per serving:  206 calories, 6.5g fat (sat 1.7g), 50mg cholesterol, 19.6g protein, 17.2g total carbohydrate (3.4g fiber, 4.7g sugar), 753mg sodium

# Burrito Bowl Lettuce Cups

Kid-Friendly

Serves 4
Prep Time: 10 minutes
Cook Time: 5 minutes

**Ingredients**
1 tablespoon olive oil
1 lb. ground beef (90% lean)
1 15-oz. can black beans
1 cup beef broth
1 tablespoon lime juice
1 head butter lettuce, separated into lettuce cups
Optional: hot sauce, sliced green onions, guacamole, black olives, limes

*Spice mix:*
1 tablespoon cumin
2 teaspoons chili powder
2 teaspoons garlic powder
1 ½ teaspoons salt
1 teaspoon oregano
¼ teaspoon black pepper

**Directions**
Combine all spice mix ingredients in a small bowl. Select the Sauté setting on the Instant Pot and heat the olive oil. Add the ground beef and spice mix, and sear the meat until very well-browned, 8-10 minutes. Add the beans, beef broth, and lime juice and stir well.

Press Cancel to reset the cooking method. Lock the lid and set the Pressure Release to Sealing. Select the Manual or Pressure Cook setting and set the cooking time to 5 minutes at high pressure.

Once the timer goes off, let sit for at least 10 minutes; the pressure will release naturally. Then switch the Pressure Release to Venting to allow any last steam out.

Open the lid and taste, adding salt, pepper, or hot sauce to your taste. If you prefer the filling to be drier, select the Sauté setting and allow the liquid to cook down for 5-10 minutes. Serve the burrito filling scooped into lettuce cups with your favorite burrito toppings.

Nutrition per serving:  391 calories, 15.9g fat (sat 5.3g), 72.8mg cholesterol, 33.6g protein, 28.7g total carbohydrate (10.5g fiber, 0.9g sugar), 1408mg sodium

# Simplest Beef Stroganoff

Kid-Friendly
20 Minutes or Less

Serves 4
Prep Time: 10 minutes
Cook Time: 18 minutes

**Ingredients**
1 tablespoon all-purpose flour
1 teaspoon salt
¼ teaspoon pepper
1 lb. beef stew meat (bottom round), cut into ½-inch strips
1 tablespoon olive oil
1 medium onion, chopped
3 cloves garlic, minced
1 cup white mushrooms, sliced
3 tablespoons red wine vinegar
1 cup beef broth

**Directions**
In a large bowl, mix the flour, salt, and pepper. Add the beef strips and toss to coat well. Select the Sauté setting on the Instant Pot and heat the olive oil. Shake any excess flour from the beef and sauté until well-browned. Add the remaining ingredients to the Instant Pot.

Press Cancel to reset the cooking method. Lock the lid and set the Pressure Release to Sealing. Select the Meat/Stew setting and set the cooking time to 18 minutes at medium pressure.

Once the timer goes off, let sit for at least 10 minutes; the pressure will release naturally. Then switch the Pressure Release to Venting to allow any last steam out.

Open the lid and taste, adding more salt and pepper if necessary. Serve with spiralized carrots, your favorite low-carb noodles, or roasted sweet potatoes.

Nutrition per serving: 279 calories, 16.7g fat (sat 5.7g), 65.8mg cholesterol, 25.4g protein, 5.5g total carbohydrate (0.8g fiber, 1.5g sugar), 844mg sodium

# White Bean and Turkey Pesto Bowls

Kid-Friendly

Serves 4
Prep Time: 5 minutes
Cook Time: 35 minutes

**Ingredients**
1 cup dried white beans, such as great northern, cannellini, or chickpeas
1 medium onion, chopped
3 cloves garlic, minced
1 teaspoon salt
¼ teaspoon pepper
2 ½ cups beef broth
¾ lb. ground turkey
½ cup pesto

*For the pesto:*
1 cup fresh basil leaves
2 cloves garlic
2 tablespoons reduced-fat parmesan cheese, grated
2 tablespoons extra virgin olive oil
2 tablespoons beef broth, or more as needed
Salt and pepper to taste

**Directions**
In the Instant Pot, add the beans, onion, garlic, salt, pepper, and broth. Stir well and spread out the beans so that they're in an even layer and submerged in the broth. Add the ground beef in an even layer over the beans, crumbling it with your fingers as you add it.

Lock the lid and set the Pressure Release to Sealing. Select the Pressure Cook or Manual setting and set the cooking time to 35 minutes at high pressure. While the beans and beef cook, combine all pesto ingredients in a food processor or blender. If pesto is too thick, add more beef broth.

Once the timer goes off, let sit for at least 10 minutes; the pressure will release naturally. Then switch the Pressure Release to Venting to allow any last steam out.

Open the Instant Pot and taste, adding more salt and pepper if needed. Stir in the pesto, spoon into bowls, and serve warm, drizzled with additional pesto, if desired.

Nutrition per serving:  377 calories, 15.2g fat (sat 3.5g), 69.4mg cholesterol, 27.8g protein, 32.7g total carbohydrate (9.9g fiber, 2.3g sugar), 1197mg sodium

# Lone Star State Beef Chili

Kid-Friendly

Serves 4
Prep Time: 10 minutes
Cook Time: 35 minutes

## Ingredients
1 lb. ground beef (90% lean)
1 medium green bell pepper, seeded and diced
1 large onion, chopped
1 medium carrot, finely diced
¼ teaspoon black pepper
1 teaspoon salt
1 teaspoon onion powder
1 tablespoon lime juice
1 tablespoon chili powder
1 teaspoon paprika
2 teaspoons garlic powder
2 teaspoons cumin
2-14 oz. cans fire roasted tomatoes

## Directions
Select the Sauté setting, add the ground beef, and cook until browned. (For more flavor, cook the beef past browned, until it begins to sear a bit and get darker.) Add all remaining ingredients and stir well, scraping up any browned bits from the bottom of the pot.

Press Cancel to reset the cooking method. Lock the lid and set the Pressure Release to Sealing. Select the Meat/Stew setting and set the cooking time to 35 minutes at high pressure.

Once the timer goes off, use a kitchen towel or oven mitts to protect your hand and move the Pressure Release knob to Venting to perform a quick pressure release.

Open the lid and taste, adding salt, pepper, or hot sauce, if necessary. Serve over cauliflower steaks or baked potatoes, or ladle into a bowl and top with guacamole.

Nutrition per serving:  306 calories, 12.5g fat (sat 4.7g), 72.8mg cholesterol, 27.2g protein, 24.2g total carbohydrate (6.4g fiber, 3.8g sugar), 949mg sodium

# Low Calorie Instant Pot Vegetarian and Vegetable Side Recipes

# Perfect Cauliflower Mash

Kid-Friendly
7 Ingredients or Less
20 Minutes or Less

Serves 4 as a side
Prep Time: 5 minutes
Cook Time: 5 minutes

**Ingredients**
1 large head cauliflower, cored and cut in large florets
1 cup low-sodium chicken broth
3 tablespoons unsalted butter
½ tablespoon garlic powder
Salt to taste
Pepper to taste

**Directions**
Add the cauliflower and broth to the Instant Pot. Lock the lid and set the Pressure Release to Sealing. Select the Pressure Cook or Manual setting and set the cooking time to 5 minutes at high pressure.

Once the timer goes off, use a kitchen towel or oven mitts to protect your hand and move the Pressure Release knob to Venting to perform a quick pressure release.

Drain, reserving any excess broth, and return the cauliflower to the pot. With a potato masher, immersion blender, or fork, mash to your desired consistency, adding broth as needed for more moisture. Stir in the butter and garlic powder, and add salt and pepper to taste.

**Note:** For more flavor, mix in fresh herbs such as thyme or rosemary before serving. You can also stir in a splash of unsweetened original almond milk for a creamier mash.

Nutrition per serving:  141 calories, 9.1g fat (sat 5.5g), 22.6mg cholesterol, 5.6g protein, 12.6g total carbohydrate (5.4g fiber, 5.4g sugar), 107mg sodium

# 10-Minute Balsamic Roasted Beets

20 Minutes or Less
7 Ingredients or Less

Serves 6 as a side
Prep Time: 1 minute
Cook Time: 10 minutes

**Ingredients**
6 medium beets (about 2 in. in diameter), unpeeled
3 tablespoons balsamic vinegar
2 tablespoons olive oil
Salt to taste
Pepper to taste

**Directions**
Wash the beets well and remove any leaves. Add 1 cup of water to the Instant Pot and place the trivet on top. Arrange the beets on the trivet.

Lock the lid and set the Pressure Release to Sealing. Select the Pressure Cook or Manual setting and set the cooking time to 10 minutes at high pressure.

Once the timer goes off, use a kitchen towel or oven mitts to protect your hand and move the Pressure Release knob to Venting to perform a quick pressure release.

Remove the beets, allow to cool, and peel. The skin should slip off easily. Slice the beets into rounds or chop them into bite-sized pieces. Dress them with the balsamic vinegar, olive oil, and salt and pepper to taste.

Serve immediately or allow to marinate for 30 minutes for more flavor.

Nutrition per serving: 82.1 calories, 4.6g fat (sat 0.6g), 0mg cholesterol, 1.4g protein, 9.2g total carbohydrate (2.3g fiber, 6.7g sugar), 82mg sodium

# Flavor Bomb Asian Brussels Sprouts

20 Minutes or Less

Serves 4
Prep Time: 5 minutes
Cook Time: 3 minutes

**Ingredients**
¾ cup vegetable broth
3 tablespoons soy sauce
1 tablespoon rice wine vinegar
2 tablespoons sesame oil
2 teaspoons garlic powder
1 teaspoon onion powder
1 teaspoon paprika
¼ teaspoon cayenne pepper
1 tablespoon almonds, raw, chopped
2 lbs. Brussels sprouts, halved

**Directions**
In a small bowl, combine the vegetable broth, soy sauce, rice wine vinegar, sesame oil, garlic powder, onion powder, paprika, cayenne pepper, and salt. Set aside.

Select the Sauté setting and add the almonds. Stir constantly until toasted, watching them carefully so they don't burn. Spoon almonds into a small bowl and set aside. Press Cancel to turn off the Sauté setting then add the reserved sauce to the pot. Add the brussels sprouts and stir well to coat them in the sauce.

Lock the lid and set the Pressure Release to Sealing. Select the Pressure Cook or Manual setting and set the cooking time to 1 minute at high pressure.

Once the timer goes off, use a kitchen towel or oven mitts to protect your hand and move the Pressure Release knob to Venting to perform a quick pressure release.

Open the lid and taste, adding salt and pepper to taste, if necessary. Garnish with the toasted almonds and serve warm over cauliflower rice or as a side for a lean protein.

**Note:** For spicier brussels sprouts, try doubling or tripling the quantity of cayenne pepper, or add a few tablespoons of your favorite hot sauce.

Nutrition per serving:  184 calories, 8.7g fat (sat 1.2g), 0mg cholesterol, 9.2g protein, 23.2g total carbohydrate (9.2g fiber, 5.8g sugar), 733mg sodium

# Amazingly Adaptable Roasted Sweet Potatoes

Kid-Friendly
7 Ingredients or Less
20 Minutes or Less

Serves 4
Prep Time: 5 minutes
Cook Time: 7 minutes

**Ingredients**
¼ cup olive oil
4 medium sweet potatoes (about 1 ¼ lbs. total), peeled or unpeeled, in 1-inch pieces
1 teaspoon garlic powder
1 teaspoon sea salt
¼ teaspoon pepper
1 cup chicken low-sodium broth

**Directions**
Select the Sauté setting on the Instant Pot and heat the olive oil or butter. Add the sweet potatoes, salt, pepper, and garlic powder to the pot and sauté for 5 minutes, stirring constantly. Add the broth and stir well.

Press Cancel to reset the cooking method. Lock the lid and set the Pressure Release to Sealing. Select the Pressure Cook or Manual setting and set the cooking time to 7 minutes at high pressure.

Once the timer goes off, use a kitchen towel or oven mitts to protect your hand and move the Pressure Release knob to Venting to perform a quick pressure release.

Open the lid and taste, adding salt and pepper to taste, if necessary. Serve warm over a salad or as a side for chicken or another protein.

**Note:** This recipe can be adapted many ways, according to your family's tastes. Try adding a favorite spice mix, curry powder, or cayenne pepper before pressure cooking, fresh herbs like rosemary and thyme after cooking, or a drizzle of truffle oil before serving.

Nutrition per serving:  243 calories, 13.9g fat (sat 2g), 0mg cholesterol, 3.4g protein, 27.5g total carbohydrate (4g fiber, 5.7g sugar), 671mg sodium

# Simplest Brothy Beans

Kid-Friendly
7 Ingredients or Less

Serves 4
Prep Time: 5 minutes
Cook Time: 35 minutes

**Ingredients**
1 lb. dried white beans, such as great northern, cannellini, or chickpeas
1 medium yellow onion, quartered
2 celery stalks, cut in half
1 medium carrot, peeled and cut in half
8 cups water
Salt to taste
Freshly ground pepper to taste
Extra virgin olive oil to taste
1 lemon, juiced

**Directions**
In the Instant Pot, add the beans, onion, celery, carrots, water, and 1 teaspoon of salt. Lock the lid and set the Pressure Release to Sealing. Select the Pressure Cook or Manual setting and set the cooking time to 35 minutes at high pressure.

Once the timer goes off, let sit for at least 10 minutes; the pressure will release naturally. Then switch the Pressure Release to Venting to allow any last steam out.

Open the Instant Pot and season beans generously with salt and pepper, tasting the broth as you add seasoning until it's to your taste. Serve warm, drizzled with a few drops of olive oil and lemon juice.

Nutrition per serving: 399 calories, 1.7g fat (sat 0.4g), 0mg cholesterol, 24.2g protein, 74.4g total carbohydrate (29.1g fiber, 2.3g sugar), 622mg sodium

# Southern Stewed Greens

7 Ingredients or Less
20 Minutes or Less

Serves 4 as a side
Prep Time: 10 minutes
Cook Time: 5 minutes

**Ingredients**
¼ lb. bacon, in 1-inch pieces
5 cloves garlic, roughly chopped
2 large bunches collard greens (about 4 cups), de-stemmed and roughly chopped
3/4 cup low-sodium chicken broth
Salt to taste
Pepper to taste
Optional: 1 tablespoon apple cider vinegar

**Directions**
Select the Sauté setting and add the bacon, cooking until it has rendered its fat and crisped up, 5-7 minutes. Add the garlic and cook, stirring constantly, for 1 minute. Add the greens, broth, and salt and pepper to taste. You may need to add the greens in batches, stir, and allow to wilt slightly until it all fits in the pot.

Press Cancel to reset the cooking method. Lock the lid and set the Pressure Release to Sealing. Select the Pressure Cook or Manual setting and set the cooking time to 5 minutes at high pressure.

Once the timer goes off, use a kitchen towel or oven mitts to protect your hand and move the Pressure Release knob to Venting to perform a quick pressure release.

Open the lid, taste, and add more salt and pepper if necessary. If desired, stir in 1 tablespoon of apple cider vinegar to add brightness to the dish. Serve warm.

Nutrition per serving: 175 calories, 13.4g fat (sat 4.3g), 19mg cholesterol, 6.6g protein, 8.7g total carbohydrate (1.4g fiber, 0.1g sugar), 422mg sodium

# Sage and Garlic Spaghetti Squash

20 Minutes or Less
7 Ingredients or Less

Serves 4
Prep Time: 5 minutes
Cook Time: 15 minutes

**Ingredients**
1 large spaghetti squash (about 5 lbs.)
2 tablespoons olive oil
5 garlic cloves, minced
1 tablespoons fresh sage, chopped
1 teaspoon salt
1/8 teaspoon nutmeg
Pepper to taste

**Directions**
Halve the squash and scoop out any seeds. In the Instant Pot, add 1 cup of water and place the trivet inside. Arrange the two squash halves on the trivet so that the flesh side is facing up. This can either be done side-by-side or stacked on top of each other, depending on the size of your squash and your Instant Pot.

Lock the lid and set the Pressure Release to Sealing. Select the Pressure Cook or Manual setting and set the cooking time to 7 minutes at high pressure.

As the squash pressure cooks, heat the olive oil in a small skillet. Add the garlic, sage, salt, nutmeg, and pepper to taste. Cook until fragrant, 2-4 minutes. Set aside.

Once the timer goes off on the Instant Pot, let sit for at least 10 minutes; the pressure will release naturally. Then switch the Pressure Release to Venting to allow any last steam out.

Remove the squash from the Instant Pot and use a fork to shred the flesh into spaghetti-like strands. Toss with the garlic sage oil, add salt and pepper to taste, and serve warm.

Nutrition per serving: 241 calories, 10g fat (sat 1.6g), 0mg cholesterol, 3.9g protein, 40.3g total carbohydrate (0.3g fiber, 0.1g sugar), 677mg sodium

# Balsamic and Garlic Stewed Kale

20 Minutes or Less
7 Ingredients or Less

Serves 4 as a side
Prep Time: 5 minutes
Cook Time: 4 minutes

## Ingredients
1 tablespoon olive oil
5 cloves garlic, roughly chopped
2 large bunches kale (about 4 cups), de-stemmed and roughly chopped
1 cup low-sodium chicken broth
Salt to taste
Pepper to taste
3 tablespoons balsamic vinegar

## Directions
Select the Sauté setting and heat the olive oil. Add the garlic and cook, stirring constantly, until fragrant, 3-5 minutes. Add the kale, broth, and salt and pepper to taste.

Press Cancel to reset the cooking method. Lock the lid and set the Pressure Release to Sealing. Select the Pressure Cook or Manual setting and set the cooking time to 4 minutes at high pressure.

Once the timer goes off, use a kitchen towel or oven mitts to protect your hand and move the Pressure Release knob to Venting to perform a quick pressure release.

Open the lid and add the balsamic vinegar. Taste and add more salt and pepper if necessary. Serve warm.

Nutrition per serving: 89 calories, 4.2g fat (sat 0.6g), 0mg cholesterol, 3.7g protein, 10.7g total carbohydrate (1.4g fiber, 1.9g sugar), 341mg sodium

# Easiest Baked Sweet Potatoes

Kid-Friendly
7 Ingredients or Less

Serves 4
Prep Time: 1 minute
Cook Time: 20 minutes

**Ingredients**
4 medium sweet potatoes (about 1 ¼ lbs. total)

**Directions**
Place the Instant Pot trivet inside the pot. Prick the potatoes all over with a fork to allow them to vent. Arrange potatoes in one layer on top of the trivet and add 1 cup of water to the pot.

Lock the lid and set the Pressure Release to Sealing. Select the Steam setting and set the cooking time to 20 minutes at high pressure.

Once the timer goes off, let sit for at least 10 minutes; the pressure will release naturally. Then switch the Pressure Release to Venting to allow any last steam out.

Carefully remove the hot potatoes and serve warm.

Nutrition per serving:  112 calories, 0.1g fat (sat 0g), 0mg cholesterol, 2g protein, 26.2g total carbohydrate (3.9g fiber, 5.4g sugar), 71.5mg sodium

# Low Calorie Sauces and Seasonings

# Low Calorie Lemon Pepper Seasoning

Kid-Friendly
7 Ingredients or Less
20 Minutes or Less

Prep Time: 5 Minutes
Cook Time: 0 minutes

**Ingredients**
6 lemons, zested
2 teaspoons garlic powder
1 tablespoon freshly cracked black pepper
2 teaspoons salt

In a small bowl, combine all ingredients. Store in a tight-sealing container in the refrigerator and use on chicken, fish, vegetables, and more.

Nutrition per recipe: 51 calories, 0.4g fat (sat 0.1g), 0mg cholesterol, 2.1g protein, 13.8g total carbohydrate (6g fiber, 2.9g sugar), 4657mg sodium

# Low Calorie Taco Seasoning

Kid-Friendly
7 Ingredients or Less
20 Minutes or Less

Prep Time: 2 Minutes
Cook Time: 0 minutes

**Ingredients**
2 tablespoons chili powder
1½ tablespoons ground cumin
2 teaspoons garlic powder
¼ teaspoon cayenne pepper
1 teaspoon dried oregano
2 teaspoons salt
1 teaspoon black pepper

In a small bowl, combine all ingredients. Store in a tight-sealing container at room temperature and use on chicken, fish, meat, sweet potatoes, vegetables, and more.

Nutrition per recipe: 109 calories, 4.8g fat (sat 0.6g), 0mg cholesterol, 4.7g protein, 18.4g total carbohydrate (7.7g fiber, 2.7g sugar), 4820mg sodium

# Low Calorie Italian Seasoning

Kid-Friendly
7 Ingredients or Less
20 Minutes or Less

Prep Time: 2 Minutes
Cook Time: 0 minutes

**Ingredients**
1 tablespoon garlic powder
½ tablespoon dried oregano
1 teaspoon dried basil
1 teaspoon dried thyme
1 teaspoon salt
1 teaspoon black pepper

In a small bowl, combine all ingredients. Store in a tight-sealing container at room temperature and use on chicken, fish, meat, sweet potatoes, vegetables, and more.

You can also make a delicious Italian dressing by adding olive oil and apple cider vinegar to this seasoning and shaking well. This makes a healthy, gluten-free, sugar-free Italian dressing that can be used to marinate chicken, fish, and pork or can be drizzled over roasted vegetables.

Nutrition per recipe: 41 calories, 0.4g fat (sat 0.1g), 0mg cholesterol, 1.9g protein, 9.2g total carbohydrate (2.6g fiber, 2.1g sugar), 2329mg sodium

# Low Calorie Indian Spice Mix

Kid-Friendly
7 Ingredients or Less
20 Minutes or Less

Prep Time: 2 Minutes
Cook Time: 0 minutes

**Ingredients**
2 tablespoons curry powder
2 tablespoons cumin
2 teaspoons turmeric
2 teaspoons ground coriander
1 teaspoon ground ginger
½ teaspoon cinnamon

In a small bowl, combine all ingredients. Store in a tight-sealing container at room temperature and use on in curries or on chicken, fish, meat, sweet potatoes, vegetables, and more.

Nutrition per recipe: 132 calories, 5.7g fat (sat 0.7g), 0mg cholesterol, 5g protein, 21.8g total carbohydrate (9g fiber, 0.9g sugar), 31.2mg sodium

# Cooking Times for the Instant Pot Electric Pressure Cooker

The Instant Pot and other electric pressure cookers are miracle workers for cutting down on calories while keeping the flavor in your life. I've included the suggested cooking times for a wide range of foods here. You can check the calorie count of nearly any food with a quick online search or on the Myfitnesspal app.

This list will also prove useful for feeding family members who aren't going watching calories or aren't trying to reduce how much fat and carbohydrates they eat. With an electric pressure cooker like the Instant Pot, you can cook up nearly a week's worth of meal-building staples in just a few minutes. That way, your family can still eat the things they enjoy, even while you opt out (from both eating them *and* cooking them nightly!).

Keep these times handy for anytime you need a simple staple ingredient done quickly.

**A note on cooking beans and other legumes in the Instant Pot:**
Dried beans will double in volume after cooking, so never fill your electric pressure cooker more than halfway and be sure to fully cover the beans with liquid.

| Dried Beans, Legumes, and Lentils | DRY Cooking Time (minutes) | SOAKED Cooking Time (minutes) |
|---|---|---|
| Black beans | 20 – 25 | 6 – 8 |
| Black-eyed peas | 10 – 15 | 4 – 5 |
| Chickpeas (chickpeas, garbanzo beans) | 35 – 40 | 10 – 15 |
| Cannellini beans | 30 – 35 | 8 – 10 |
| Great Northern beans | 25 – 30 | 8 – 10 |
| Kidney beans, red | 25 – 30 | 8 – 10 |
| Kidney beans, white / Cannellini | 30 – 35 | 8 – 10 |
| Lentils, green | 10 – 12 | n/a |

| | | |
|---|---|---|
| Lentils, brown | 10 – 12 | n/a |
| Lentils, red, split | 5 – 6 | n/a |
| Lentils, yellow, split (moong dal) | 18 – 20 | n/a |
| Lima beans | 12 – 14 | 8 – 10 |
| Navy beans | 20 – 25 | 7 – 8 |
| Pinto beans | 25 – 30 | 8 – 10 |
| Peas | 6 – 10 | n/a |

| Meat | Cooking Time (mins) |
|---|---|
| Beef, stew meat | 20 / 450 gm / 1 lb |
| Beef, meatballs | 8-10 / 450 gm / 1 lb |
| Beef (pot roast, steak, rump, round, chuck, blade or brisket), small pieces | 15 / 450 gm / 1 lb |
| Beef (pot roast, steak, rump, round, chuck, blade or brisket), large pieces | 20 / 450 gm / 1 lb |
| Beef, ribs | 20 – 25 |
| Beef, shanks | 25 – 30 |
| Chicken, breasts (boneless) | 6 – 8 |
| Chicken, whole 2-2.5 Kg | 8 / 450 gm / 1 lb |
| Chicken, cut with bones | 10 – 15 |
| Chicken, bone stock | 40 – 45 |
| Ham, slices | 9 – 12 |
| Ham, picnic shoulder | 8 / 450 gm / 1 lb |

| | |
|---|---|
| Lamb, cubes | 10 – 15 |
| Lamb, stew meat | 12 – 15 |
| Lamb, leg | 15 / 450 gm / 1 lb |
| Pork, loin roast | 20 / 450 gm / 1 lb |
| Pork, butt roast | 15 / 450 gm / 1 lb |
| Pork, ribs | 15 – 20 |
| Turkey, breast (boneless) | 7 – 9 |
| Turkey, breast (whole) | 20 – 25 |
| Turkey, drumsticks (leg) | 15 – 20 |
| Veal, chops | 5 – 8 |
| Veal, roast | 12 / 450 gm / 1 lb |

# Guidelines for Buying Organic Produce and Whole Foods

While buying organic isn't essential to a low-calorie diet, it is a good way to rid your diet of any trace pesticides or other chemicals that can also cause inflammation and digestive problems. Buying organic can be expensive, but we all want to feed our families the healthiest and safest fruits and vegetables. That's where the Dirty Dozen and Clean Fifteen come in.

Each year, the Environmental Working Group issues its Shopper's Guide to Pesticides in Produce, which ranks the pesticide contamination of popular fruits and vegetables. Rankings are based on data from more than 35,200 samples which are tested each year by the U.S. Department of Agriculture and the Food and Drug Administration.

The top 15 types of produce that have the least amount of pesticide residue are known as the Clean Fifteen, while the top 12 most contaminated fruits and vegetables are called the Dirty Dozen.

By knowing which fruits and vegetables contain more pesticides and which contain less, you can make more informed choices and stretch your grocery dollar further.

**The Dirty Dozen**
*When possible, buy these organic.*

1. Strawberries
2. Spinach
3. Nectarines
4. Apples
5. Grapes
6. Peaches
7. Cherries
8. Pears
9. Tomatoes
10. Celery
11. Potatoes
12. Sweet Bell Peppers
13. Hot Peppers

**The Clean Fifteen**
*These do not need to be bought organic.*

1. Avocados
2. Sweet Corn
3. Pineapples
4. Cabbage

5. Onions
6. Sweet peas
7. Papayas
8. Asparagus
9. Mangos
10. Eggplant
11. Honeydew Melon
12. Kiwi
13. Cantaloupe
14. Cauliflower
15. Broccoli

# Metric Conversion Charts

If you use metric measurements in your cooking, use these handy charts to convert the recipes in this book to work in your kitchen. You can also find a free and easy-to-use metric conversion calculator at: https://www.convert-me.com/en/convert/cooking or with a quick online search.

| | | | |
|---|---|---|---|
| 1/4 tsp | = 1 ml | | |
| 1/2 tsp | = 2 ml | | |
| 1 tsp | = 5 ml | | |
| 3 tsp | = 1 tbl | = 1/2 fl oz | = 15 ml |
| 2 tbls | = 1/8 cup | = 1 fl oz | = 30 ml |
| 4 tbls | = 1/4 cup | = 2 fl oz | = 60 ml |
| 5 1/3 tbls | = 1/3 cup | = 3 fl oz | = 80 ml |
| 8 tbls | = 1/2 cup | = 4 fl oz | = 120 ml |
| 10 2/3 | = 2/3 cup | = 5 fl oz | = 160 ml |
| 12 tbls | = 3/4 cup | = 6 fl oz | = 180 ml |
| 16 tbls | = 1 cup | = 8 fl oz | = 240 ml |
| 1 pt | = 2 cups | = 16 fl oz | = 480 ml |
| 1 qt | = 4 cups | = 32 fl oz | = 960 ml |

33 fl oz  =  1000 ml  =  1 l

| | | | |
|---|---|---|---|
| **Freeze Water** | 32° F | 0° C | |
| **Room Temp.** | 68° F | 20° C | |
| **Boil Water** | 212° F | 100° C | |
| **Bake** | 325° F | 160° C | 3 |
| | 350° F | 180° C | 4 |
| | 375° F | 190° C | 5 |
| | 400° F | 200° C | 6 |
| | 425° F | 220° C | 7 |
| | 450° F | 230° C | 8 |

# Helpful Resources

If you'd like to learn more about a low-calorie diet and the Instant Pot electric pressure cooker, I highly recommend these books:

*The Essential Instant Pot Cookbook: Fresh and Foolproof Recipes for Your Electric Pressure Cooker* by Coco Morante

Available for purchase here: http://bit.ly/essentialinstantpotbook

*Dinner in an Instant: 75 Modern Recipes for Your Pressure Cooker, Multicooker, and Instant Pot* by Melissa Clark

Available for purchase here: http://bit.ly/dinnerinaninstant

*The Skinnytaste Cookbook: Light on Calories, Big on Flavor* by Gina Homolka

Available for purchase here: http://bit.ly/skinnytaste

*Instant Loss Cookbook: Cook Your Way to a Healthy Weight with 125 Recipes for Your Instant Pot, Pressure Cooker, and More* by Brittany Williams

Available for purchase hre: http://bit.ly/instantloss

# Did you find these recipes helpful?

## If so, would you consider paying it forward by leaving a review on Amazon?

A review is the best way to help me spread the word about this book, and hopefully it will help the next person find their way to healthier, easier low-calorie Instant Pot meals, too!

**To leave a review:**

Type this URL into your browser: http://bit.ly/skinnyinstantpot

OR:

Google search "skinny instant pot cookbook Lauren Smythe" and click the first Amazon link.

This should take you to the Amazon book page, where you can leave a review.

**Thank you so much!**

# Gift a book = give a meal!

We believe everybody deserves a warm, healthy meal to come home to. That's why we've committed to donating one meal to a family in need through Feeding America for each copy sold of this book. So just by purchasing a copy of this book, you've helped feed a neighbor in need— thank you so much for that.

To spread the love even more, you can also gift a copy of this book to a friend. They'll love you for it, and you'll be making a difference in another family's life!

**To gift a book:**

Type this URL into your browser: http://bit.ly/skinnyinstantpot

OR:

Google search "skinny instant pot cookbook Lauren Smythe" and click the first Amazon link.

This should take you to the Amazon book page, where on the right, you'll see a button that says "Give as a Gift."

**Happy gifting!**

39857660R00060

Made in the USA
Middletown, DE
21 March 2019